# The Principal's Guide to RAISING MATH ACHIEVEMENT

## CORWIN
## PRESS

**The Corwin Press logo**—a raven striding across an open book—represents the happy union of courage and learning. We are a professional-level publisher of books and journals for K–12 educators, and we are committed to creating and providing resources that embody these qualities. Corwin's motto is "Success for All Learners."

# The Principal's Guide to RAISING MATH ACHIEVEMENT

## Elaine K. McEwan

CORWIN PRESS, INC.
A Sage Publications Company
Thousand Oaks, California

*For information:*

Corwin Press, Inc.
A Sage Publications Company
2455 Teller Road
Thousand Oaks, California 91320
E-mail: order@corwinpress.com

Sage Publications Ltd.
6 Bonhill Street
London EC2A 4PU
United Kingdom

Sage Publications India Pvt. Ltd.
M-32 Market
Greater Kailash I
New Delhi 110 048 India

Printed in the United States of America

*Library of Congress Cataloging-in-Publication Data*

McEwan, Elaine K., 1941–
     The principal's guide to raising math achievement /
by Elaine K. McEwan.
          p.   cm.
     Includes bibliographical references and index.
     ISBN 0-8039-6784-5 (cloth: acid-free paper)
     ISBN 0-8039-6785-3 (pbk.: acid-free paper)
     1. Mathematics—Study and teaching—United States—
Evaluation.   I. Title.
     QA13 .M315   2000
     510′.71′073—dc21                                    00-008086

This book is printed on acid-free paper.

     01   02   03   04   05   06   7   6   5   4   3   2

| | |
|---|---|
| *Corwin Editorial Assistant:* | Kylee Liegl |
| *Production Editor:* | Denise Santoyo |
| *Editorial Assistant:* | Victoria Cheng |
| *Typesetter/Designer:* | Lynn Miyata |

# Contents

# Preface

ach fall, a new class of 5-year-olds enters our public schools—eager, bright-eyed, and hopeful that the mysteries of letters and numbers will be unlocked for them.

Each spring another graduating class marches across the platform to receive their high school diplomas, many far less eager and hopeful than they were in kindergarten. We've "had" these students for 13 or 14 years, and too many have failed to reach the levels of literacy and numeracy that will enable them to succeed in higher education, in work, even in life. We've lost count of how many never make it to "Pomp and Circumstance."

Reading was my first passion, and I have turned the educational spotlight on literacy in every educational position I have held. As a classroom teacher, a learning center teacher/librarian, an elementary school principal, and, finally, an assistant superintendent for instruction, I was relentless in my pursuit of reading and writing proficiencies for all students, but especially for those who came to school without the background and readiness to read: those students who spoke another language, were poor and hungry, or whose hours were filled with violent television shows rather than nursery rhymes and picture books.

Since retiring from public education, I have written *The Principal's Guide to Raising Reading Achievement* (1998) and have introduced hundreds of principals in both the United States and Canada to the need for research-based reading curricula, well-trained teachers, and strong instructional leadership. Reading is still my passion, but I have also become increasingly distressed by another critical problem in our schools—innumeracy. The mathematical version of illiteracy is just as widespread and serious as its reading counterpart, but, unfortunately, it's not a cause that spouses of politicians or professional basketball players adopt and promote. Innumeracy is rarely mentioned in presidential speeches, and we do not have a Mathematics Is Fundamental Foundation. Our failure to produce numerate graduates is as much a national disgrace as our illiteracy rate, but we can more easily sweep innumeracy under the carpet. After all, we have calculators and computers to compensate for our mathematical gaps. Unfortunately, while technology may enable us to cope with the more mundane mathematical demands of life, it can't supply "the appreciation and understanding of information which is presented in mathematical terms, for instance, in graphs, charts, or tables, or by references to percentage increase or decrease. [Technology] can't help us understand the ways in which mathematics can be used as a means of communication" (Cockcroft, 1982).

In 1983 I became an elementary school principal in a small district, kindergarten through eighth grade, in the suburbs of Chicago. Although the district was home to affluent areas where upwardly mobile young executives moved their growing families into burgeoning subdivisions, my school fronted on railroad tracks in the central downtown. The building was old, the playground was rusty, and the paint in the hallways was fading and peeling—a fitting backdrop for a demoralized veteran faculty. The standardized test scores in both math and reading were abysmal. Students in grades 2 through 6 as a group were at the 20th percentile in reading and the 17th percentile in math on the Iowa Test of Basic Skills. We tackled reading achievement first, with great success. With each succeeding year we reduced the number of students who scored in the bottom quartile. Our scores jumped to the 60th, 70th, and even the 80th percentile in reading. But we soon realized that we could not neglect our math deficiencies.

We discovered that the majority of our sixth-grade students failed the junior high school math proficiency test. They were doomed to the low math track for the rest of their academic careers. They would never master algebra, the "gatekeeping" course to advanced learning. Even the doors of our local community college would be closed to them unless we drastically improved student achievement. We determined that it wasn't enough to give our students literacy; we had to provide numeracy as well.

In the eight years I served as building principal, student achievement in mathematics rose as dramatically as it did for reading. The junior high school mathematics chairperson noticed the trends. "What are you doing over there?" she wondered. "We're phasing out remedial math classes and adding another section of fast-paced math for next year. It's all because of you," she added with a twinkle in her eye.

I smiled broadly, pleased that our efforts were not going unnoticed. "We're doing a lot of things," I explained. "Raising expectations for students, focusing on outcomes, eliminating repetitious review, introducing math competitions, and holding teachers accountable for student achievement." I shared the details of our school-business partnership with the George J. Ball Company, an international seed company located in our attendance area. A team of Ball plant pathologists assisted our upper-grade faculty and students in designing experiments to investigate the effects of varying amounts of light and types of fertilizers on germination rate and plant productivity. Our classrooms became greenhouses and our students became researchers. When the experiments were concluded, the junior scientists reported their findings to a standing-room-only audience of scientists and corporate executives. Then we raised our expectations to an even higher level: the application of our students' learning to a real-world problem—profit and loss.

Since the students had documented the optimum conditions for growing beautiful flowers in our classrooms, the faculty conceived the idea of forming mini-greenhouses to grow and sell plants. The students selected what they believed would be the most marketable plants, purchased the seed from Ball, cultivated several varieties, marketed the flowers with a vigorous advertising campaign, and held a block-buster Mother's Day Plant Sale. Mathematics achievement includes both the mastery of foundational skills and the application of those skills outside of the classroom. We found that although the ability to retrieve facts automatically and a mastery of basic algorithms and mathematical rules were essential, we also needed to provide opportunities for what researchers at the Consortium on Chicago School Research call "authentic intellectual work" (Newmann , Lopez, & Bryk, 1998, p. 15).

The critical issues surrounding mathematics achievement are coming to the forefront in the popular press. The United States' poor showing in the Third International Mathematics and Science Study (International Association for the Evaluation of Educational Achievement, 1997) is hard to ignore. Who is responsible for changing this disturbing trend? We educators. As instructional leaders of our schools, we must make a difference, one student at a time.

I have written *The Principal's Guide to Raising Math Achievement* with these goals in mind: (a) to convince you of the power that rests in you and your faculty to make numeracy a reality for each of your students; (b) to introduce you to the current controversies in math instruction; (c) to set forth some of the most recent research in mathematics instruction so that you and your faculty can make informed decisions; and (d) to share with you how you can change what you're doing to make a powerful difference.

Raising achievement is never easy, but the controversy that currently swirls around mathematics and how best to teach it makes the administrator's task even more challenging. We need to become as informed as possible about the issues, the research, and, most particularly, about what materials and methods have the potential to produce the achievement we desire for all of our students. We are often totally dependent on subject matter coordinators, teacher training institutions, and national organizations to guide our thinking and practice. When we are confronted by teachers or parents who question or possibly disagree with the recommendations of the experts, we are often forced to defend practices we do not fully understand while also being held accountable for low or declining achievement that we feel powerless to influence. If you have experienced this dilemma, you are not alone. I, and many others, have walked in your shoes.

*The Principal's Guide to Raising Math Achievement* is based on a number of strong personal beliefs. My goal is to engage your thinking and assist your decision making. I hope that by setting forth my beliefs at the outset I will provide a meaningful context in which you can place my recommendations about mathematics instruction. Regarding the 1989 National Council of Teachers of Mathematics (NCTM) Standards, I have concerns. I am hopeful that the updated standards to be issued in 2000 will include changes that reflect the input and revisions suggested by professional mathematicians, parents, NCTM members, and classroom teachers who have implemented the standards for a decade. I share the feelings of the Learning First Alliance, whose members have recommended submitting comments regarding the revision of the 1989 NCTM Standards. They assert that "the assessment and curriculum structure framework should be influenced by research in mathematics education, including what is done in other countries with successful mathematics education programs" (Learning First Alliance, 1998, p. 13). I regard many of the standards-based textbooks and programs with a healthy degree of skepticism. I believe that results, not good intentions, are what matter most. I believe that professional educators have an obligation to pay attention to what our consumers—parents and taxpayers—feel is important in education. I believe we have a responsibility to communicate with our constituencies in language that is free of jargon and respects the knowledge and expertise of consumers. I believe that achievement is important. I believe that norm-referenced tests are essential for accountability. I believe that students learn best with structure, discipline, and effective instruction. I am not a mathematician, a math educator, or a math researcher. I approach this topic as an administrator who is charged with raising mathematics achievement in my school, as the individual who bears the ultimate responsibility for the bottom line. I approach the topic looking for what works.

## Who This Book Is For

This book has been written for several audiences. It is primarily intended for school principals at every level to help them develop a plan for raising mathematics achievement in their schools. New administrators and administrators without a background in math instruction or curriculum will find it especially helpful. It can also be used by mathematics specialists and central office administrators who are evaluating mathematics programs for kindergarten through 12th grade and formulating district improvement goals. Finally, it can serve as a valuable resource for school improvement teams as they grapple with what needs to change in their schools. *The Principal's Guide to Raising Math Achievement* can also serve as a source of information for mathematics educators at the college and university level as they seek to make their classroom experiences more relevent to practitioners.

## What This Book Is Not

*The Principal's Guide to Raising Math Achievement* is designed to help you explore possibilities, philosophies, and controversies so that you might be better prepared to exercise instructional leadership. It is not an instructional guide, and it does not contain specific strategies or "can do's" for classroom teachers to use in raising math achievement. The recipe or magic bullet for raising math achievement that you may be searching for does not exist. School improvement initiatives need to be rooted in a school's culture and climate and are better framed by a team of teachers in response to the challenges posed by the community and its students. There are answers to the problems of low or declining achievement, but they require study and intellectual application on the part of you and your faculty.

## Overview of the Contents

Chapter 1 explores the current state of mathematics achievement in the United States and suggests some of the reasons why our students as a whole don't compare more favorably with their international counterparts. Chapter 2 provides background and history on mathematics education. The great debate in reading has a counterpart in mathematics instruction—the "math wars." In order to make informed decisions about instruction and curriculum in your school, you must understand the key issues in this sometimes acrimonious discussion.

Chapter 3 examines the need for research-based decision making in education. "It costs no more to use a tested reform than an untested innovation. But unproductive innovations waste not only money but also the effort of school personnel and the hard work of children trying to excel" (Carnine, 1993, p. 40). If you are going to commit your energy and resources to change, make sure you know how to evaluate the claims that a program or innovation is "research-based." Chapter 4 focuses on what Benjamin

Bloom (1980) calls the "alterable variables," the things that you and your faculty *can* and *must* change in order to bring students to acceptable levels of numeracy. Too often, educators focus on inalterable variables like students' backgrounds or parents' educational levels and fail to recognize how much they really do control. You are introduced to six alterable variables, then given concrete, research-based suggestions about how to change the status quo in your school. Chapter 5 focuses on the "essential learnings" that constitute a comprehensive mathematics curriculum for kindergarten through 12th grade. These "essentials" are critical regardless of what program or textbooks you choose. Chapter 6 describes the key components that need to be in place to create a "numerate" school. You'll investigate instructional leadership, shared decision making, planning and goal setting, parental involvement, a well-designed accountability system, and a reasonable improvement time line. Finally, Chapter 7 provides more than 30 ideas you can implement in your school to raise mathematics achievement. There are Web sites for teachers, activities and programs for students, and ways for you, the principal, to become more involved in raising mathematics achievement.

I hope that after reading *The Principal's Guide to Raising Math Achievement* you will be motivated to set about raising mathematics achievement in your school. Changing the attitudes, achievement, and accountability of your students and teachers with regard to mathematics may require some changes on your part as well. It is never too late to become more mathematically literate yourself. Exercise your instructional leadership and creativity to lead your faculty and students to new levels of numeracy!

## *Acknowledgments*

The author would like to acknowledge the following reviewers:

Frank Allen, Ph.D.
Professor Emeritus of mathematics, Elmhurst College (IL); former president of the National Council of Teachers of Mathematics

Richard H. Escobales, Jr., Ph.D.
Professor of mathematics, Canisius College (NY)

David C. Geary, Ph.D.
Professor of psychology, University of Missouri; author of *Children's Mathematical Development* and contributor to the *Mathematics Framework for California Public Schools*

Ralph A. Raimi, Ph.D.
Professor Emeritus of mathematics, University of Rochester (NY); coauthor of *State Mathematics Standards: An Appraisal of Math Standards in 46 States, the District of Columbia, and Japan,* Thomas B. Fordham Foundation.

Gerald Rising, Ph.D.
Professor of mathematics, State University of New York at Buffalo

Hung-Hsi Wu, Ph.D.
Professor of mathematics, University of California at Berkeley

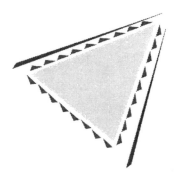

# About the Author

**E**laine K. McEwan is a partner in The McEwan-Adkins Group, an educational consulting firm. She received her B.A. degree from Wheaton College and her M.A. in Library Science and Ed.D. in Educational Administration from Northern Illinois University. She has been a teacher, librarian, elementary school principal, and assistant superintendent for instruction. McEwan is the author of more than two dozen books for parents, children, and educators, including *Attention Deficit Disorder* (1996), *Leading Your Team to Excellence: Making Quality Decisions* (1997), *When Kids Say No to School: Helping Students at Risk of Failure, Refusal, or Dropping Out* (1998), *Seven Steps to Effective Instructional Leadership* (1998), *The Principal's Guide to Attention Deficit Hyperactivity Disorder* (1998), *How to Deal with Parents Who Are Angry, Troubled, Afraid, or Just Plain Crazy* (1998), *The Principal's Guide to Raising Reading Achievement* (1998), *Ten Traits of Highly Successful Schools: How You Can Tell If Your School is a Good One* (1999), *How to Raise a Reader* (1999), and *Managing Unmanageable Students: Practical Solutions for Educators* (2000).

# Mathematics Achievement

## *Where Do We Stand?*

*"Math class is tough."*
> —Programmed statement made by the Teen Talk
> Barbie Doll. (*New York Times,* 1993, p. D1)

*"Jolene wants to purchase a television that costs $250. She has $25 now and will be able to save $15 each week. The television model has been discontinued, and the price will be reduced by $10 each week until it is sold. After how many weeks will Jolene have saved enough money to buy the television?"*
> —Maryland State Department
> of Education, 1999 [On-line]

*"Even if you are not convinced by anything else. . ., I hope that you will be convinced that our ability to use numbers is fundamental to the way we think about the world, that it is the basis of much of what we call civilization, and that to understand our common humanity we need to understand how we understand numbers."*
> —Butterworth, 1999, p. 19

Mathematics is a hard sell to many folks. Even well-educated school leaders get sweaty palms and heart palpitations when confronted with an algebra problem. They can relate to "Barbie's" anxiety about math class. Consequently, raising mathematics achievement isn't a topic that's likely to headline the faculty meeting agenda. It's hard to ignore the results of the Third International Mathematics and Science Study (TIMSS), however. Even though U.S. students scored above the international mean at the fourth-grade level, their scores were considerably lower at the eighth-grade level, and our showing at the 12th-grade level was downright dismal. On general math knowledge at the 12th-grade level, the United States placed 18th out of the 21 countries whose students took the test. Only Lithuania, Cyprus, and South Africa did worse (Schmidt, McKnight, & Raizen, 1997a).

Raising mathematics achievement has taken on an urgency in this country matched in intensity only by that period in the late 1950s when we appeared to be losing the space race with the Russians. The issue is not merely one of national pride and taking home the gold medal in mathematics, however. There are clear indicators that mathematics achievement is critical to a student's success in higher education and, ultimately, in life.

## What's So Important About Math?

Math matters. It matters big time. First, consider the impact of math proficiency on the ability and likelihood of a student's pursuing postsecondary education.

◆ Algebra is the gateway course for two-year college admission. Many of the most popular majors at two-year colleges—including business, nursing, and computer science—require rigorous mathematics coursework, such as statistics (U.S. Department of Education, 1997).

◆ Finishing a mathematics course beyond the level of algebra II more than doubles the odds that a student will get a bachelor's degree (Adelman, 1999).

◆ Eighty-three percent of students who took algebra I and geometry went on to college within two years of high school graduation. Of students who did not take algebra I and geometry courses, only 36% went on to college (U.S. Department of Education, in press).

◆ Low-income students who took algebra I and geometry were almost three times as likely to attend college as those who did not (United States Department of Education, 1997).

Mathematics proficiency and the doors it opens to higher education also make a difference in an individual's earning capacity.

"For the business community the [TIMSS] results are chilling. In an increasingly global economy where workforce quality and skill levels are critical factors in achieving success, American business requires a world-class workforce if we are to continue to lead the world's economy."
—Business Coalition for Education Reform, 1999

▶ In 1997, a college graduate with a bachelor's degree earned nearly $18,000 for every $10,000 earned by a high school graduate (U.S. Department of Labor, Bureau of Labor Statistics, 1997).

▶ Twenty-eight-year-old workers who tested in the top quartile of math skills on the National Assessment of Educational Progress earn 37% more than those in lower quartiles (U.S. Department of Labor, 1997).

In addition to the increased educational and earnings potential for students afforded by mathematics achievement, one cannot overlook the economic impact that our students' lack of knowledge and skill levels has on the United States' ability to be competitive in the global economy.

◆ A one-year increase in the education level of a company's workforce increased productivity by 8.6%. For nonmanufacturing companies the productivity increase was even higher—11.0% (National Center on the Educational Quality of the Workforce, 1995).

◆ American businesses spend more than $25 billion each year on remedial education for their employees, most of whom are products of the nation's public schools (Kearns, 1989, p. 2).

◆ Occupations that once required few skills in mathematics now call for specific skills in algebra, geometry, measurement, probability, and statistics. For example, an entry-level automobile worker needs to be able to apply formulas from algebra and physics to properly wire the electrical circuits of any car (U.S. Department of Education, 1997).

◆ Fifty percent of information technology company executives report a lack of skilled workers as "the most significant barrier" to their companies' growth (U.S. Department of Commerce, 1999).

> "It is easy to understand why people don't rush out to buy mathematical journals, poring over the latest results in the cohomology of fiber bundles. After all, mathematics does get pretty abstract and seemingly far removed from life. But it is difficult to understand why so many people must struggle with concepts that are actually simpler than most of the ideas they deal with every day. It is far easier to calculate a percentage than it is to drive a car. The notion of probability is child's play compared to the concept of a bridal shower."
> —Dewdney, 1993, p. v

As if the previous information regarding educational opportunities, earning capabilities, and the state of the U.S. economy doesn't offer enough support for the critical importance of mathematics achievement, consider the social costs of innumeracy. John Allen Paulos, in his witty volume *Innumeracy: Mathematical Illiteracy and Its Consequences* (1988), argues that "our inability to deal rationally with very large numbers or with the probabilities associated with them results in misinformed governmental policies, confused personal decisions, and increased susceptibility to pseudosciences of all kinds" (from the book jacket).

## What's the Score?

We can't be that bad, can we? What difference does it make if the Asian countries outstrip us in mathematics achievement? After all, they stress conformity, rote learning, and mindless drill of basic skills. Their children have little time for play and relaxation. At least that's the common wisdom. As a nation we like to think of ourselves as "relaxed, successful, effective individualists who are creative, innovative, and independent" (Stevenson & Stigler, 1992, p. 21). We claim Bill Gates and Steven Jobs as our own. The prevalent myths about our strengths and the weaknesses of Asian countries have often served to make us feel smug and secure in our mathematical ignorance. After all, we don't want to cultivate a nation of nerds, do we? Or do we?

We've always excused our lack of competitive math scores by pointing to our high school graduation rates, which were higher than our competitive peers in Europe and Asia. "After all," we've pontificated as a nation, "when you're educating the masses, quality will suffer a bit. But it's worth it." Unfortunately, we will no longer be able to pat ourselves on the back for even that distinction. While high school completion in the rest of the world is on the rise, the U.S. rate has declined. The United States ranks last behind other developed countries with only 72% of its 18-year-olds earning diplomas in 1996 (U.S. Department of Education, 1998).

We've also fallen back on the timeworn excuse that our country is a melting pot and that diversity is a contributing factor to our poor performance. Interestingly enough, the data from the TIMSS do not support that commonly held belief (Schmidt, McKnight, Cogan, Jakwerth, & Houang, 1999, pp. 163–164). Our perceived social heterogeneity did not translate into unusual achievement heterogeneity when that latter heterogeneity was compared to its counterparts in other countries. We can no longer blame our low math achievement on our diversity. More disappointing is that even our best students were not among the best from all the TIMSS countries (Schmidt et al., 1999, p. 177).

## What's the Problem?

Madge Goldman, a leading advocate in the private philanthropic community for the funding of basic mathematical research, harshly criticizes mathematical education in an *Education Week* commentary. "Our school systems take our bright, normal children and turn them into dummies. Mass malpractice is perpetrated by insufficiently trained teachers, further constrained by unfocused and often incoherent curricula and textbooks" (Goldman, 1998, p. 56). Before you reject Goldman's comments as an overreaction, consider the findings of researchers who have carefully examined mathematics curricula and instructional practices from countries around the world. They concluded that: "U.S. achievement variability for 9- and 13-year-olds in mathematics was not so much *nature as created*" (Schmidt et al., 1999, p. 177). In the executive summary of *A Splintered Vision: An Investigation of U.S. Science and Mathematics Education*, William Schmidt and his colleagues proffer several possible reasons for the poor overall mathematics performance of U.S. students as compared to their international peers. Highlighted in the report as serious problems are (1) unfocused and overloaded curricula; (2) textbooks that contain too many topics that are repeated over and over again from one grade level to the next; and (3) teachers who try to teach too much in too short a time with too many activities (Schmidt, McKnight, & Raizen, 1997b, pp. 3–6).

To consider how to raise mathematics achievement in your school, begin with the results of the TIMSS (Beaton et al., 1996; Mullis, et al., 1997, 1998). The TIMSS reports and summary documents are comprehensive and voluminous—nearly a thousand pages. To save you time, the key findings and their implications for your school are summarized for you in the following pages. If you do nothing else, examine the sample test items (International Association for the Evaluation of Educational Achievement, 1997). How *might* your students have scored if they *had* taken the test? Based on what you've read thus far about the role that mathematics achievement plays in a child's future, what can you prognosticate for the educational and economic futures of the students in your school? What could you as an administrator be doing to change their futures for the better? You cannot afford to leave decisions regarding mathematics instruction solely in the hands of others. Planning for change requires shared decision making, but you should always be a part of the process and preferably as the leader, not a follower.

## What Can We Learn From the TIMSS?

### What Was the Purpose of the Testing?

The TIMSS provided countries with a means for investigating what their school-age populations know and can do in mathematics and science. The test focused on "concepts students understand, how well they can apply their knowledge to problem-solving situations, and whether they can communicate their understanding" (Mullis et al., 1997, p. 9). The TIMSS evaluation also includes a videotape study of eighth-grade mathematics instruction consisting of observations in 231 classrooms in Japan, Germany, and the United States (Stigler & Hiebert, 1997), and an analysis of more than 1,100 textbooks and curriculum frameworks from nearly 50 countries (Schmidt et al., 1996; Schmidt et al., 1997).

## Who Was Tested and When Did the Testing Occur?

More than half a million students at five grade levels (3,4,7,8, and 12) from 45 countries were tested in mathematics and science in 1994 and 1995. Approximately 15,000 schools around the world were involved, and the tests were translated into 30 different languages. The primary focus of the data interpretation as well as of the demographic and attitudinal information was a summative snapshot of grades 4, 8, and 12. Students in the third and seventh grades were also tested to create a quasi-longitudinal picture of gains in learning that occurred in the fourth and eighth grades. An informative discussion of what the gain scores tell us about instruction and how the United States compares to other countries can be found in *Facing the Consequences: Using TIMSS for a Closer Look at U.S. Mathematics and Science Education* (Schmidt et al., 1999).

## Who Administered the Tests?

Research centers in each country, coordinated by the International Association for the Evaluation of Education Achievement (IEA) headquartered at Boston College, were responsible for managing the across-country tasks such as training country representatives in standardized procedures, selecting comparable samples of schools and students, and conducting the various steps necessary for data processing and analysis.

## Where Can Copies of the Actual Reports Be Obtained?

All of the international achievement reports are available in portable document format (PDF) on the TIMSS Web site at *http://wwwcsteep.bc.edu/timss*. Documents that examine the TIMSS data from the perspective of the United States can be found at both *http://nces.ed.gov/timms/publist.html* and *http://ustimss.msu.edu/*.

## Which Countries Participated?

Students from Australia, Austria, Canada, Cyprus, the Czech Republic, England, Greece, Hong Kong, Hungary, Iceland, Indonesia, Iran, Ireland, the Islamic Republic, Israel, Italy, Japan, Korea, Kuwait, Latvia, Mexico, the Netherlands, New Zealand, Norway, Portugal, Scotland, Singapore, Slovenia, Thailand, and the United States participated in the test. While the results for every country are reported, in some cases countries failed to satisfy guidelines for sample participation rates or used unapproved sampling procedures. This information is always reported for the reader. Although not every country participated at every grade level, results from the United States are available for the five grades tested.

## What Aspects of Mathematics Learning Were Tested?

Six content dimensions were covered in the TIMSS mathematics test given to primary-school students (third- and fourth-graders): whole numbers, fractions, and proportionality; measurement, estimation, and number sense; data representation, analysis, and probability; geometry; and patterns, relations, and functions (Mullis et al., 1997, p. 14).

Six content areas were covered in the mathematics test taken by seventh- and eighth-grade students: fractions and number sense; measurement; proportionality; data representation, analysis, and probability; geometry; and algebra (Beaton et al., 1996, p. 12).

At the 12th-grade level, two tests were given: (1) a mathematics literacy test designed to measure the mathematics learning of all final-year students who are at the point of leaving school and entering the workforce or postsecondary education, regardless of their school curriculum, and (2) an advanced mathematics test designed to measure learning of advanced mathematics concepts among final-year students who have studied advanced mathematics (Mullis et al., 1998, p. 13).

## What Are the Results?

Figure 1.1 summarizes the results of the elementary and middle school mathematics tests, and Figure 1.2 describes the results of the two high school tests.

There isn't much to write home about when one looks at the mathematical proficiency of students from the United States. Our high school seniors, even those who are considered to be advanced mathematics students, don't compare favorably with their international counterparts. Out of the 21 countries that participated in the secondary literacy test for all students, the United States came in 18th. Of the sixteen countries whose students took the test for advanced mathematics students, we ranked 15th. The results appear even more dismal when one considers that the Asian countries that dominated the elementary and middle school tests (Singapore, Korea, Japan, and Hong Kong) didn't even participate in the secondary study. The best runners weren't even in the race—and we still brought up the rear. Although our elementary and middle school students had more acceptable performance levels, the mean scores of the United States were still statistically significantly lower than the Asian countries at all grade levels. We also had a notably smaller percentage of students scoring in the top quartile as compared to the four top-scoring countries.

*"Our curricula, textbooks, and teaching all are 'a mile wide and an inch deep'."*
—*Schmidt et al., 1997b, p. 2*

## Why Isn't the United States More Competitive?

The experts are hard at work to learn why we lag so far behind other countries of the world in mathematics achievement. Schmidt and his colleagues at the U.S. National Research Center for the TIMSS have published three volumes that discuss data from their analysis of 491 curriculum guides and 628 textbooks from around the world (1996, 1997a, 1997b). In the executive summary of the study, they assert that "there is no one at the helm of mathematics and science education in the United States; in truth, there is no identifiable helm. No single coherent vision of how to educate today's children dominates U.S. educational practice in either subject, nor is there a single commonly accepted place to turn for such visions. Our visions to the extent that they exist at all are multiple" (Schmidt et al, 1997b, p. 1).

**FIGURE 1.1.**
Summary of TIMSS Data: Elementary and Middle Schools

| Grade Level | | Mean Scores of Four Top-Scoring Countries/ Percentage of Students Scoring in Top Quartile | Percentage of U.S. Students Scoring in Top Quartile | Ranking of US Mean Score Compared to Total Participating Countries |
|---|---|---|---|---|
| Intl. Mean | US Mean | | | |
| Grade 3 | 480* | Korea 561/36 Singapore 552/32 Japan 538/24 Hong Kong 524/17 | 8 | 10th out of 24 participating countries |
| 470 | | | | |
| Grade 4 | 545* | Singapore 625/39 Korea 611/26 Japan 597/23 Hong Kong 564/18 | 9 | 12th out of 26 participating countries |
| 529 | | | | |
| Grade 7 | 476* | Singapore 601/44 Korea 577/34 Japan 571/31 Hong Kong 564/30 | 7 | 23rd out of 39 participating countries |
| 484 | | | | |
| Grade 8 | 471* | Singapore 643/45 Korea 607/34 Japan 605/32 Hong Kong 565/27 | 5 | 28th out of 41 participating countries |
| 500 | | | | |

NOTE: * Mean achievement is significantly lower than top scoring countries. This significance is at the .05 level, adjusted for multiple comparison.
Adapted from Mullis, I. V. S., Martin, M. O., Beaton, A. E., Gonzalez, E. J., Kelly, D. L., & Smith, T. A. (1997, June). *Mathematics Achievement in the Primary School Years: IEA's Third International Mathematics and Science Study (TIMSS)*, pp. 24-25, 28-29, 33-34; and from Beaton, A. E., Mullis, I. V. S., Martin, M. O., Gonzalez, E. J., Kelly, D. L., & Smith, T. A. (1996, November). *Mathematics Achievement in the Middle School Years: IEA's Third International Mathematics and Science Study (TIMSS)*, pp. 22-23, 26-27, 31-32.

Every group has its own solution to the problem of low mathematics achievement in the United States—the business community, the academic think tanks, the politicians, the National Council of Teachers of Mathematics, professional mathematicians, and publishers of mathematics textbooks. But as an administrator, you are far more concerned about what's happening in your school than in the rest of the country. You care about the learning of the students who are enrolled in your school today. You don't have time to wait for a vision from on high. You need answers now. Perhaps the problem in your school is the same one that plagues our country on a grand scale—it's suffering from a splintered vision. The standards, curricula, textbooks, tests, and teachers are like pieces from different puzzles. No matter how hard you try, you can't make them fit into a complete picture. Who is responsible for creating a seamless and coherent vision in your school? You are, with the help of your staff members and parent community.

**FIGURE 1.2.**
Summary of TIMSS Data: Secondary Schools

| Test | U.S. Mean Score | Int'l Mean Score | Mean Scores of Four Top-Scoring Countries† Ranking of U.S. mean Score Compared to Total Number of Participating Countries | Ranking of U.S. Mean Score Compared to Total Number of Participating Countries |
|---|---|---|---|---|
| Mathematics literacy achievement test for all graduating students | 461*‡ | 500 | Netherlands 560<br>Sweden 552<br>Denmark 547<br>Switzerland 540 | 18th out of 21 participating countries |
| Advanced mathematics test for students who had taken or were taking precalculus, calculus, or AP calculus | 442*‡ | 501 | France 557<br>Russian Federation 542<br>Switzerland 533<br>Australia 525 | 15th out of 16 participating countries |

NOTE: Adapted from Mullis, I.V.S., Martin, M. O., Beaton, A. E., Gonzalez, E. J., Kelly, D. L., & Smith, T. A. (1998, February). *Mathematics and Science Achievement in the Final Year of Secondary School: IEA's Third International Mathematics and Science Study (TIMSS)*. pp. 33, 46-47, 128-129.

†The top-scoring countries in the elementary and middle school testing (Singapore, Korea, Japan, and Hong Kong) did not participate in the secondary school testing.

*Mean achievement is significantly lower than the *four top-scoring countries*. This significance is at the .05 level, adjusted for multiple comparisons.

‡Mean achievement is significantly lower than the *international mean*. This significance is at the .05 level, adjusted for multiple comparisons.

## What Can You Do?

The good news is that there are answers out there. You need not feel frustrated and powerless. In the chapters ahead you'll find information, ideas, resources, and research to help you work with your staff to bring about significant improvement in mathematics achievement. Before you roll up your sleeves and get down to the nitty-gritty of figuring out what needs to be changed, however, take time for a brief history lesson. Santayana (1905–1906/1982) warned that "those who cannot remember the past are condemned to repeat it" (p. 423). In no arena does that quote have more relevance than in education. We seem to ride the curricular and instructional pendulums back and forth, seldom learning from our past mistakes. Chapter 2 summarizes where we've been in math education and what the current controversies are. Armed with understanding, you will be better able to avoid the pitfalls of the past and lead your school to mathematical excellence.

# The Math Wars

## Drill Versus Discovery

*"As the pendulum swings from one magic solution to another each decade gets its name: The 'back to basics' 1950s; the 'New Math' 1960s; the 'back to basics' 1970s; the 'problem solving' 1980s; and the 'group learning' 1990s. What makes a splash depends a good deal on the passion of some articulate, dedicated speaker willing and able to spread the gospel of reform at conferences or on the availability of grants from foundations or the government. Someone has to be convinced that he or she has found the key to successful mathematics education."*

—Stein, 1996, p. 76

The swirling discussions and debates regarding mathematics education are enough to give administrators vertigo. Wherever one turns, whether it is to the popular press, the education press, or a mathematics journal, how we ought to be teaching mathematics is a hot topic. How did a discipline known for its precise definitions, neat formulas, and right answers become the center of so much controversy? The conflict is symptomatic of one that has dogged educators since the turn of the century—the traditionalists versus the progressivists. Do we value the product or the process? Do teachers have a body of knowledge that is worth transmitting to students, or do children construct their own learning through real-world experiences?

"Math instruction in the United States has oscillated between the same poles that shape and reshape our culture, politics, and even our morality. We are torn between discipline and liberation, between demanding performance and handing out praise—a two-step dance that in education causes us to fixate on facts and formulas and then to turn around and complain that rote learning undermines understanding" (Colvin, 1999a, 4).

Unfortunately, we don't have a stellar track record in mathematics reform and achievement; the more we change, the more we seem to stay the same. In the inaugural volume of *The Mathematics Teacher,* published in 1908, a frustrated teacher wrote: "One of the most obvious facts about mathematics in our secondary schools is a general dissatisfaction which is expressed on all sides. . . . There is an alarming number of failures, especially in the first year of high school. . . . Instructors in colleges and universities rarely miss an opportunity for declaring that their students come poorly prepared. The programs of teachers' meetings and the tables of contents of pedagogical journals are teeming with titles which assume that something is wrong" (Lennes, 1908, p. 94). Here we are, nearly 100 years later, and the same thing could be said: One of the most obvious facts about mathematics in our schools is a general dissatisfaction. In this new millennium, however, the dissatisfaction includes a far broader group of individuals than just the teachers. CEOs, politicians, parents, and policy makers have joined the ranks of the dissatisfied.

## Are We Condemned to Repeat the Past?

The history of mathematics education during the first half of the 20th century was relatively uneventful. Oh, there were a few creative experiments—like the one conducted by a brave superintendent in Manchester, New Hampshire. He decided to postpone arithmetic instruction until the sixth grade and spend the extra class time in reading, reason, and reciting, theorizing that so little new content was actually taught from year to year in mathematics, he could compact the curriculum and accomplish the same goals in a shorter period of time. After sending notes to parents about the experiment and hearing no objections, he implemented the plan. The findings didn't surprise the superintendent. The students whose mathematics instruction was delayed until sixth grade achieved as well or better than those who had been studying the subject since third grade. He reported the results of his highly successful, albeit controversial experiment in a series of articles in the *Journal of the National Education Association* (Benezet, 1935a, 1935b, 1936) with a brief aside that explained how he had pulled off his radical experiment: the parents of his carefully selected experimental group were unable to read and speak English. His research caused scarcely a blip on the educational radar screen.

Mathematics reform in the late 1950s was more exciting, and I was a firsthand observer and eager participant. The Russians launched Sputnik, and, overnight, math and science achievement came under fire for its shortcomings. American scientists and mathematicians were recruited to turn things around, and the Honors Institute for Young Scientists was established in Grand Rapids, Michigan. High school students were identified, I among them, to participate in a summer-long enrichment program. University professors from around the country became our instructors in mathematics, chemistry, and physics. We took field trips to state universities and enjoyed hands-on experiences in well-equipped laboratories and classrooms. It was heady stuff for a high school student. I can't remember much of what I learned that summer, other than a healthy respect for how much I didn't know.

In 1958 the School Mathematics Study Group (SMSG) was formed. Mathematicians, teachers, and teachers of teachers worked side by side to hammer out textbooks that were tested in hundreds of classrooms. Among the more revolutionary instructional ideas to emerge from this reform movement was the idea of teaching students in bases other than 10. By the time the "new math" textbooks hit the classrooms, I was a fifth-grade teacher struggling to explain to doubtful parents and confused students how this curricular innovation would "deepen [students'] understanding of the decimal notation for whole numbers. In using a new base [other than 10], [students] must look at the reasons for carrying and the other mechanical procedures in a new light and gain deeper insight into the decimal system" (Stein, 1996, p. 84).

Dubbed the "new math" by a growing cacophony of critics, the work of the SMSG disappeared, not as quickly but just as completely as Benezet's experiment in the hamlets of New Hampshire. The parents didn't buy it. They couldn't help their kids with homework. They didn't see the point. The pendulum once again swung back to the basics, but the reformers were waiting in the wings. The NCTM issued its *Agenda for Action* in 1980. Its number one recommendation was to make problem solving the focus of instruction (NCTM, 1980). Work on new standards for mathematics instruction began shortly thereafter and the NCTM Standards were unveiled in 1989.

## The 1989 NCTM Standards

The 1989 NCTM Standards were launched with an ambitious agenda—to provide the national vision for teaching mathematics that was lacking in the United States. Our international peers were at a distinct advantage. Their students and teachers were all on the same page. With national curricula and textbooks, their instruction was more uniform and better focused. In the United States, there were as many different curricula, textbooks, and methodologies as there were states, school districts, and teachers of mathematics. If Student A living in California graduated with the same mathematical knowledge as Students B and C living in Texas and Florida, it was by accident rather than by design.

The NCTM, hoping to rally the entire country around its plan, outlined five goals for students: (1) to value mathematics; (2) to become confident in their ability to do mathematics; (3) to become mathematical problem solvers; (4) to learn to communicate mathematically; and (5) to learn to reason mathematically (NCTM, 1989, pp. 5–6). To accomplish these goals, the authors selected four themes: (1) mathematics as problem solving; (2) mathematics as communication; (3) mathematics as reasoning; and (4) mathematical connections (NCTM, 1989, p. 11).

Writing in January 1993, Chester Finn described the reception the NCTM Standards received. "Even in the faddy world of K–12 education, the 'standards' issued by the National Council of Teachers of Mathematics have met with rare acceptance. Seldom has so profound a change in conventional wisdom and standard practice had such homage paid to it, so little resistance shown to its onrush, so few doubts raised about its underpinnings. Republican, Democrat, textbook publisher, and test maker, governor and businessman, federal official and local school member—just about everyone is rushing to implement the NCTM Standards. What's more, they're ceaselessly cited as the example par excellence of what national standards should look like" (Finn, 1993 [On-line]).

I was once again right in the middle of math reform. As assistant superintendent for instruction in a small suburban school district, I was charged with forming a committee to choose a new math series. The NCTM Standards arrived in the mail just before our first meeting. Not stopping to think about how teachers would help each child construct the knowledge that was said to be a personal matter for each learner, I quickly photocopied some key pages and handed them out. I wanted our district to be on the cutting edge. The committee members embraced the ideas enthusiastically. They were eager to find materials to support these lofty goals. We became part of the rush to jump on the NCTM bandwagon.

But there were those on our committee who had second thoughts. As they looked at a now well-known and very popular standards-based series, which at the time was still in its developmental phase, they voiced the same doubts that Jeremy Kilpatrick expressed in an editorial in the *Journal for Research in Mathematics Education* in 1988. Kilpatrick was skeptical, as were some of my committee members, about the radical shift that was being proposed. "The working draft of the NCTM's *Curriculum and Evaluation Standards for School Mathematics* argues forcefully for a de-emphasis in skill instruction and for a change in the apparently widespread view that proficiency needs to precede, and perhaps to dominate comprehension and problem solving. Although researchers may agree with the draft position—and many undoubtedly do—they should not dismiss too lightly the question of how and where skill development fits into the school mathematics curriculum. Recent research in cognitive science suggests that a strong knowledge base is needed for problem solving, and surely some of that base should be composed of procedural knowledge" (Kilpatrick, 1988, p. 274).

As my committee and I discovered in 1990–91, textbook publishers were still scrambling to produce programs that matched the 1989 NCTM Standards. Standards-based textbooks and curricula for every grade level began to appear almost overnight. Programs like *Mathland, Everyday Mathematics, Investigations in Number, Data, and Space, Math Trailblazers, College Preparatory Mathematics, Interactive Mathematics Program,* and the *Core-Plus Mathematics Project* were produced by publishers and developed through funding from the National Science Foundation. As these NCTM standards–based textbooks made their way into classrooms around the country, opinions regarding the standards suddenly shifted from stupendous to suspect, and the first volley was fired in the "math wars."

## The Math Wars

The math wars had their official beginning in 1995. Dr. Michael McKeown, a molecular biologist at the Salk Institute in San Diego, and his wife, Erica Heikoff McKeown, a former math teacher and professional mathematics tutor, became alarmed at the lack of mathematics content in the *College Preparatory Mathematics* textbook their twins were scheduled to use in algebra. They met with the appropriate teachers and administrators to make their concerns known, only to be told that "nobody uses the math you learned any more" (Michael McKeown, personal communication, August 1, 1999). The McKeowns and a variety of other respected mathematicians and scientists in the Southern California area begged to differ regarding the "usefulness of their math" and founded Mathematically Correct, an organization devoted to "the concerns raised by parents and scientists about the invasion of our schools by the 'new-new math' and the need to restore basic skills to math education" (Mathematically Correct, 1997).

Similar backlash movements from parents regarding the implementation of standards-based programs erupted across the state of California (e.g., Escondido, Palo Alto, and Torrance). While California's math wars have garnered a high-profile national audience (Sommerfeld, 1996, April 24 [On-line]; West, 1995, June 7 [On-line]), similar controversies regarding standards-based math curricula can be found in Texas (Bell, 1999, August 25, p. 1); Massachusetts (Concerned Parents of Reading); Oregon (Kremer, 1998); and in the Department of Defense Schools (McArthur, November, 1999 [On-line]).

The wars have been widely chronicled in a broad spectrum of media. E. D. Hirsch, author of *The Schools We Need and Why We Don't Have Them* (1996), offered his perspective on the NCTM approach to teaching mathematics in a *Time* magazine article. "It doesn't work, it doesn't comport with reliable theories, and we're making a mistake" (Ratnesar, 1997, pp. 66–67).

*Newsweek* magazine quoted Jack Price, a professor of mathematics education at California State Polytechnic University at Pomona and a former president of the National Council of Teachers of Mathematics. He labeled the traditional approach advocated by Hirsch and Mathematically Correct as "nostalgia math" (Kantrowitz, 1997, p. 62).

John Leo, a commentator for *U.S. News and World Report*, took a satirical approach in his treatment of the math wars, describing a greeting card he had recently seen. The card read: *"Instead of having 'answers' on a math test, they should just call them 'impressions,' and if you got a different 'impression,' so what, can't we all be brothers?"* (Leo, 1997, p. 14).

Weekly newsmagazines weren't the only ones covering the math wars. In an *Education Week* commentary, Tom Loveless, associate professor at Harvard University, characterized the conflict as the second great math rebellion. "When reformers seize control of the policy agenda, whether at the local, state, or national level, they almost always go too far in embracing the new, unproven practices they favor. Not only is the baby thrown out with the bath water, but the baby and the bath water are frequently replaced by something bizarre" (Loveless, 1997 [On-line]).

An article in the *School Administrator* offered some advice to practitioners about how to avoid getting caught in the line of fire. Assistant Superintendent Jayme B. Arner, the Escondido, California, administrator who was in charge of curriculum during the math battle there, warned her colleagues: "No longer are educators the unchallenged experts. When schools want to make major changes in instruction, they need to first listen carefully to the community with an open mind. Administrators need to do their homework. They need to research the math battles in other communities, including Escondido. That seems professionally proactive and wise" (Colvin, 1999a [On-line]).

*Phi Delta Kappan* devoted a substantial portion of its January 1999 issue to the mathematics debate. Thomas O'Brien (1999) offered several hypotheses to explain what it is about standards-based math that gets critics so hypercharged. "Parrot math [the phrase used by O'Brien to refer to the rote recitation of math facts] reflects a deep-seated longing to control children through external rewards and punishments, rather than to harness children's urge to make sense of things." Another possibility O'Brien suggested for the "tempest in a teapot" is that "the issue is a useful battering ram for advancing political candidates at the expense of teachers and educational leaders" (p. 2).

In the same issue of *Phi Delta Kappan*, Michael Battista (1999) summarized the feelings of many math educators regarding the antistandards movement. "Recent newspaper and newsmagazine articles, public debates at local school board meetings, and even the California State Board of Education have aimed a great deal of criticism at the current 'reform movement' in mathematics education. Exploiting the growing 'talk show/tabloid' mentality of Americans, opponents of reform support their arguments with hearsay, misinformation, sensationalism, polarization, and conflict as they attempt to seize control of school mathematics programs and return them to traditional teaching—that is, to the 'basics.' As they cite isolated examples of alleged failures of mathematics reform, they ignore countless failures of traditional curricula. Their arguments lack understanding both of the essence of mathematics and of scientific research on how students learn mathematics" (pp. 42–44).

Battista's and O'Brien's statements might be more supportable if there weren't so many respected professional mathematicians and scientists among those who questioned the 1989 NCTM Standards and continue to question the direction of mathematics education. Frank Allen, a former president of the NCTM and Professor Emeritus of Mathematics at Elmhurst College, taught high school mathematics for more than 35 years. He had this to say about the 1989 NCTM Standards in a speech to high school mathematics department chairpersons in the western suburbs of Chicago: "Most of the major recommendations have nothing to support them other than the consensus of the authors and the conventional wisdom harbored by some of our more vocal mathematics educators. How dare these writers propose sweeping changes, including a complete restructuring of the school mathematics curriculum, on such flimsy evidence?" (Allen, 1997).

We are now aware that not every member of NCTM supported the Standards, but in 1989 it appeared that support was unanimous. "Dissent from the Standards has been meager, primarily because NCTM discourages any criticism of it. If one is not for the Standards, one must be against good mathematics, good teaching, and good evaluation. . . . There is virtually no memory in the Standards of what has been recommended before and failed, and no indication of what, if anything, is truly new in the Standards. Many of its [the NCTM's] recommendations were never tested on a large scale. . . . Although support for change in mathematics education is based in great part on the low performance of U.S. students in international comparisons, the Standards have not taken the best ideas from what is done in other countries. The curricula elsewhere have been ignored. Why? One reason is that these curricula do not follow the philosophy in the Standards. Elsewhere they do not believe that children always have to construct knowledge for themselves" (Usiskin, 1994, p. 19).

Mathematics education professor Fran Curcio, in the February 1999 issue of *Mathematics Teaching in the Middle School,* accuses the critics of the reform efforts of "latching onto certain myths" in voicing their comments and points out that, contrary to what the critics assert, (1) basic computation is not being ignored; (2) correct answers are important; (3) there are many ways to teach mathematics; (4) not all so-called standards-based textbooks are created equal; and (5) there's plenty of research to support reform efforts (pp. 1–3).

Where did these myths Curcio describes come from? No doubt some of them sprang straight from recommendations in the 1989 Standards that called for decreased attention kindergarten through grade 4 to "complex paper and pencil computations, the isolated treatment of paper and pencil computations, and paper and pencil fraction computation (NCTM, 1989, p. 21). In Grades 5 through 8, the Standards called for "decreased attention for practicing tedious paper and pencil computations, finding exact forms of answers, and memorizing formulas, procedures, facts, and relationships" (NCTM, 1989, p. 71).

Some of the myths may actually have arisen from the NCTM's own Research Advisory Committee, which made the following statement in 1988 about the draft version of the 1989 Standards on which many current textbooks are based: "The Standards document contains many recommendations, but, in general, it does not provide a research context for the recommendations even when such a context is available. For which curricular and instructional recommendations made in the draft version of the Standards document [the statement applies with equal force to the final version] does there exist substantial research support?" (p. 339).

The State<br>of the<br>Standards<br>in the New<br>Millennium

The NCTM has taken seriously many of the questions raised by educators, policy makers, and their own members regarding the 1989 Standards. The writing committee went back to the table and developed a set of revised standards, *Principles and Standards for School Mathematics: Discussion Draft.* The document, which is more than 300 pages, was released in October 1998. It addressed some of the criticisms of the earlier standards. Almost two years in the writing, the *Draft* contained more content and specificity, although not nearly enough to please all the critics (Hoff, 1998).

To be a school administrator today is to be caught in the crossfire of the math wars—trying to figure out whether to run, duck, or fight. Essential to making sense of this issue is wrestling with the critical question of how students acquire mathematical learning. With "traditional" math instruction is it possible for a student to become numerate and even go on to become a professional mathematician or scientist? Or is traditional instruction to blame for poor math achievement? Must mathematical understanding be constructed by the student through meaningful situated experiences and activities? Or can some key learnings be mastered as a result of more direct instruction?

How Do<br>Students<br>Learn<br>Mathematics?

Although many of the battles in the math wars *are* being fought in school board meetings and curriculum committees, there are bloody skirmishes going on in the pages of esoteric journals as well. Cognitive psychologists, constructivist philosophers, mathematics educators, and pure mathematicians debate the issue and boggle the minds of the poor practitioner with their jargon. Experts toss about the terms *cognitivism* and *constructivism* as though their mere incantation will serve to immediately validate or denigrate any curriculum or instructional methodology under scrutiny.

At the very least, a cursory understanding of these perspectives is essential. Simplistically, cognitivism and contructivism can be compared to the opposing camps of the combatants in the math wars—the drill-and-kill camp and the camp that favors guiding children to construct their own meaning—but the two perspectives are far more complex than drill versus discovery. The answer clearly does not lie in an either/or approach.

Geary, professor of psychology and contributor to the state of California's mathematics framework, has labeled the two points of view or mindsets from which one can approach the current mathematics debate as the *mechanistic* approach and the *organismic* approach (1994, pp. 262–266). "The basic assumption of the mechanistic approach [used by many cognitive psychologists, particularly those who specialize in information processing theory, and behaviorists] is that the learner receives information from the environment, most notably the teacher—the 'sage on the stage.' The information results in reflexive changes in the child's overt behavior, such as the number of problems solved correctly, or in the child's mental representations of mathematical information" (p. 262).

The constructivist perspective that dominated the contents of the 1989 NCTM Standards and subsequent curriculum development looks at teaching and learning very differently—in an organismic way. The basic assumption of constructivism is that children are active learners and must construct mathematical knowledge for themselves. The teacher acts more as a "guide on the side" to facilitate learning, rather than lecturing and imparting skills and knowledge, that is, acting as the "sage on the stage" (Cobb, Yackel, & Wood, 1992; Lampert, 1990). In the words of one constructivist, "It is possible for students to construct for themselves the mathematical practices that, historically, took several thousand years to evolve" (Cobb et al., 1992, p. 28). Constructivists reject the results of drill and reinforcement in producing a desired behavior, refusing to concede that any simultaneous conceptual development might be occurring as a result of the acquisition of basic skills through practice. Even if drill and reinforcement do work, they are not worth considering, according to the constructivists. As von Glaserfeld, an influential radical constructivist, puts it, "The really effective teachers, of course, have always known—at least since Socrates—that examples, drill, and overt reinforcement are quite effective in producing a desired behavior; but precisely because they were good teachers they also knew that generating *understanding* was a worthier educational objective than merely modifying behavior" (von Glaserfeld & Steffe, 1991, p. 95).

Von Glaserfeld's radical views have had a profound impact on the direction of mathematics education in the United States, an impact that is rather remarkable when one considers he is neither mathematician, educator, nor researcher. He has spent 20 years developing theoretical models, and his theory of radical constructivism has shaped the thinking of many of the movers and shakers in the mathematics education community. Despite the fact that his fundamental theories have never been thoroughly tested in the crucible of the classroom, the most "radical" aspect of von Glaserfeld's theory has gained widespread support among mathematics educators and subsequently in the NCTM 1989 Standards: "Radical constructivism starts from the assumption that knowledge, no matter how it is defined, is in the heads of persons. . . . What we make of experience constitutes the only world we consciously live in. But all kinds of experience are essentially subjective, and though I may find reasons to believe that my experience may not be unlike yours, I have no way of knowing that it is the same" (von Glaserfeld, 1995, p. 1).

You may be mumbling to yourself, "I can see some validity in both approaches; at the very least a sane balance of the two is necessary. Kids absolutely need fluency and facility with math operations. They can't stop to construct meaning with manipulatives every time they need to know how much they'll save if the CD they want to buy is discounted 20%. The more facts and information children have in working memory, the more fluent and automatic their problem solving will be."

"But, on the other hand," you reason, "what good are the facts and memorized equations if a young person doesn't understand how to solve real problems in the context of everyday life?"

In a very practical and common sense discussion of how children learn mathematics, Geary (1994) summarizes this issue. "Cognitive development is very complex and involves mechanistic as well as organismic changes. To be sure, there is much to be gained by understanding social contextual influences on mathematical development (e.g., Saxe, 1991), but to assume that all development follows this route and to reject outright the idea that there are mechanistic changes in children's cognitive growth is naïve. Moreover, in addition to building basic skills, mechanistic approaches to mathematics tasks probably do influence children's conceptual development" (pp. 263–264). Geary questions just how effective any achievement initiative can be if it focuses exclusively on constructivist methodologies. "The processes that facilitate the acquisition of conceptual knowledge appear to differ from those processes that facilitate the acquisition of more mechanical skills (Sweller, Mawer, & Ward, 1983). The constructivist approach focuses on the former, but at the expense of the latter. Because of this, constructivism is not likely to lead to substantial long-term improvements in the mathematical skills of American children" (p. 266).

Cognitive psychologist John Anderson and his colleagues (Anderson, Reder, & Simon, 1995 [On-line]) at Carnegie Mellon University set forth a more balanced view of how students and teachers interact during learning:

1. Learning requires a change in the learner, which can only be brought about by what the learner does. The activity of a teacher is relevant to the extent that it causes students to engage in activities they would not otherwise engage in.

2. The task is to design a series of experiences for students that will enable them to learn effectively and to motivate them to engage in the corresponding activities.

3. When students cannot construct knowledge for themselves, they need some instruction. There is very little positive evidence for discovery learning, and it is often inferior. In particular, it may be costly in time, and when the search is lengthy or unsuccessful, motivation commonly flags.

4. People are sometimes better at remembering information that they create for themselves than information they receive passively, but in other cases they remember as well or better information that is provided than information they create.

5. Real competence only comes with extensive practice. The instructional task is not to "kill" motivation by demanding drill, but to find tasks that provide practice while at the same time sustaining interest. There are a number of ways to do this, for instance, by "learning-from-examples" (p. 12).

When, if ever, all the arguments and discussion are said and done, you will still be accountable for the mathematics achievement of your students. The time has come to tackle the nitty-gritty of raising mathematics achievement. And there has never been a more exciting time to go about this task. Despite the controversies and conflicts, we do know a lot about what kinds of programs and instruction produce results. Working with teachers, parents, and curriculum developers, we can do a better job than we have been doing. The research is the first place to look for answers. What can those who examine the critical issues in both experimental and qualitative ways tell us about how to change? Chapter 3 will help you gain an understanding of how to evaluate this research.

# Research-Based
# Decision Making

*"[N]ew theories of education are introduced into schools every day (without labeling them as experiments) on the basis of their philosophical or common sense plausibility but without genuine empirical support. We should make a larger place for responsible experimentation that draws on the available knowledge. It deserves at least as large a place as we now provide for faddish, unsystematic and unassessed informal experiments or educational reforms. We would advocate the creation of an FEA, an analogy to the FDA, which would require well-designed clinical trials for every educational drug that is introduced into the market place."*

—Anderson et al., 1995, p. 18

*"The research-to-practice pipeline has sprung many leaks."*

—Miller, 1999, p. A17

How does one usually make a decision to change? Whether the decision is to buy a new car or to implement a new mathematics curriculum, the possible reasons are often similar.

We change because it's time to change. My father bought a new car every two years if he needed one or not. In the case of my former school district, we had a school board policy that mandated a seven-year textbook adoption cycle. Every seven years, we did something new, whether it was necessary or not.

Sometimes we change because everyone else is changing and we don't want to be thought of as old-fashioned or behind the times. We buy a new car because our old one, although mechanically reliable and with nary a scratch or a spot of rust, looks out of date. In education, the competition to be on the cutting edge is fierce, so we follow the leaders without regard for where they might be taking us.

The best reason to change is not because of the passage of time or a desire to be innovative, but because we have assessed the situation and determined something is broken that needs to be fixed. In the case of our auto analogy, perhaps the repair bills are mounting and cost-effectiveness dictates the purchase of a more reliable vehicle. In mathematics education, it is time to change when a needs assessment or a program evaluation tells us that student achievement in mathematics is low or that too many students are dropping out of mathematics.

When it comes to buying that new car, you no doubt do some research. You may investigate performance records, check out ratings, and talk to people who own the models you're considering. You gather as much information as you can, evaluate its reliability and validity, then make your decision. The counterpart in education to this kind of careful consumer investigation is education research. Educators aren't particularly attracted to the research of their discipline, however. They are often guilty of making curriculum and instruction decisions based more on the "innovation du jour" than on reliable research. Many educators, myself included, have often been naïve and gullible when it comes to making decisions about what programs and methods to use in our schools. "In education, untested fads sweep through the profession, gathering authority by the number of schools using them, not by proven gains in learning. The field does not distinguish between innovations which merely create change, and reforms which are changes that yield improvements in student achievement" (Carnine, 1993, p. 40).

Why is it so difficult for some educators to use research as a basis for decisions about change? Three of the reasons have to do with our own shortcomings. First, we can blame some of our research avoidance on lack of training. Many of us weren't adequately taught how to tell the difference between good research and poor research. We may be impressed by something simply because it has been published, and, as a result, we don't ask tough questions of the author. Second, we're overloaded and overworked. We have to think on our feet. When staff members want quick decisions from us, we seldom take the time to do the research that is necessary to make an informed decision.

A third reason for the all-too-common research avoidance syndrome is a lack of numeracy. Administrators are no different than most of the citizenry—our quantitative reasoning skills could use some fine-tuning. Gina Kolata, a science reporter for the New York Times, interprets scientific research for the readers of the newspaper; she finds most readers to be very gullible when it comes to numbers. She describes a Princeton, New Jersey, school board meeting in which board members were informed by administrative staff that a review of 64 studies, which was cited in the Association of Supervision and Curriculum Development's *Educational Leadership* journal (Pavan, 1992), clearly supported the use of nongraded programs. Kolata observed that "[it] sounds impressive, but what exactly did those 64 studies consist of? Maybe they are of the highest quality, but the point is that the quality of those 64 studies was not addressed. The number was" (Kolata, 1997, p. 25).

In addition to the difficulties that educators have understanding the research, problems are inherent in the research itself. Education research is not easily categorized and assimilated. "There are so many alternative paradigms in education research that we're not really agreed upon what knowledge counts and what's good research," says Penelope L. Peterson, the dean of the school of education and social policy at

Northwestern University (Viadero, 1999, p. 33). Further complicating the issue is the number of disciplines *doing* education research. Do you want an anthropological, psychological, mathematical, or educational perspective on how children learn mathematics? Take your pick. We have some of each. Would you like a hypothetico-deductive (quantitative) or an inductive (qualitative) paradigm from which to consider the issue? We can offer you a nice selection in any size or color you prefer. We also have plenty of opinion and pseudoresearch to confuse the issue even more.

A final problem confronting us has to do with the quality of the research. Henry Levin of Teachers College, Columbia University, points out that "it's not qualitative versus quantitative. It's good research versus bad research, and the qualitative field opens up a lot more possibilities for bad research" (Viadero, 1999, p. 34). Not only do we educators need to *consult* the research before we commit to spending our human and economic resources, we also need to *evaluate* its quality. "The enthusiasm and energy of new teachers quickly become transformed into dissatisfaction and cynicism when they are caught up in a cycle of requirements to use untested innovations that, ironically, replace older failed changes. Veteran teachers find themselves labeled 'afraid of change' and 'burned out' when they recognize some of today's reforms to be relabeled experiments that have already failed in the past" (Carnine, 1993, p. 40).

Whether you are presented with a piece of research from a prestigious journal, with an article from a professional administrator's magazine, or with an evaluation summary provided by a textbook or software company, your reaction should be the same. Read it carefully to determine if what you are reading is true research or a generation of theory and opinion. Theories and opinions are highly useful—indeed, necessary—in suggesting ideas for possible investigation and in stimulating creative thinking about what could or might be, but they are not research. Articles and papers containing opinion and theory provide neither the statistical and descriptive information found in excellent quantitative research nor the rich, long-term, in-depth analysis found in a true qualitative study. "Research is the disciplined search for knowledge," and whether you carry out this search using a deductive paradigm (the scientific/experimental method) or an inductive paradigm (the qualitative method), there are criteria for judging quality (Smith & Glass, 1987, p. 6).

## Quantitative Research

Quantitative research uses statistical methods to show relationships between variables. There are two types of quantitative research: explanatory and descriptive.

### Explanatory Research

Explanatory research is considered by most to be the gold standard of education research, particularly when it has been replicated on a large scale and in many different settings. There are two types of explanatory research: experimental and quasi-experimental.

#### Experimental Research

Experimental research uses the scientific method of inquiry to test a hypothesis based on theory. A well-conceived and precisely executed experimental study has the potential to demonstrate a cause-and-effect relationship between two variables. The hypothesis is tested using one or more statistical methodologies, then analyzed to determine its "truth." Ideally, the research is reviewed by others in the field, replicated by still others, then subjected to further testing in long-term or follow-up studies. Researchers ask the question: Is a given effect the result of a particular cause? "To establish the claim that one variable is indeed the cause of another, three conditions have to be met. First, a statistical relationship between the two variables must be demonstrated. Second, the presumed cause must occur before the presumed effect. Third, all other possible causes of the presumed effect must be ruled out" (Smith & Glass, 1987, p. 125). True experimental research, as opposed to quasi-experimental research, requires the random assignment of subjects to treatment groups and control groups (i.e., groups that receive no treatment).

Be cautious about basing curricular decisions that will have an impact on large numbers of students on a one-shot case study, or, as it is currently known, action research, in which a single group (e.g., one classroom) is given some treatment presumed to cause change. The one-shot case study is neither experimental nor acceptable as a basis for drawing any meaningful conclusions. "It seems well-nigh unethical at the present time to allow, as theses or dissertations in education, case studies of this nature [i.e., involving a single group observed at one time only]" (Campbell & Stanley, 1963, p. 7).

A second type of research often assumed to be experimental research is what Campbell and Stanley (1963) call the "static-group comparison" (p. 12). One group gets a treatment and the other group doesn't, and the group that shows the most progress wins. The big problem with static-group comparison research is that there is no way of determining whether the groups were equivalent in the first place.

### Quasi-Experimental Research

Quasi-experimental is the term used to describe research studies "in which the purpose is to establish a cause-and-effect relationship between an independent variable and a dependent variable, but assignment of subjects to treatment conditions is not at random" (Cook & Campbell, 1979). There are many ways to compensate for the lack of random assignment (e.g., doing pre- and posttests), but great care must be taken in the interpretation of the results.

## Descriptive Research

Descriptive research establishes the existence of a phenomenon or describes a pattern of relationships, but does not answer questions about cause and effect. Descriptive research is quantitative, but is nonexperimental in nature. The two major types of descriptive research are surveys and evaluations.

### Survey Research

Survey research examines and describes characteristics or variables that are present in one sample of a larger population. The TIMSS study is an outstanding example of survey research in education.

**Evaluation**

Evaluation, the second type of descriptive research, is sometimes called applied research. "Evaluation is the process of establishing value judgments based on evidence about a program or product" (Smith & Glass, 1987, p. 30). "The distinction between [experimental] research and evaluation lies in the intent and purpose of the investigator" (p. 33). The experimental researcher has a need to know for knowledge's sake. The evaluator has a mission in mind: to determine if a program, methodology, or curriculum is working. Evaluation informs decision making. Experimental research is not necessarily better than evaluation, just different. In fact, evaluation, although its motives are narrow in focus, may have more widespread applications.

*Indicators of Quality Quantitative Research*

Educators need both experimental research and descriptive research in the form of evaluation. In the area of mathematics education, for example, we need to understand learning theory as it applies to children and mathematics, but we also need stringent evaluations of textbooks and teaching methodologies. Ellis and Fouts (1997) suggest three groups of questions to ask whenever one is considering the adoption of a new program.

1. What is the theoretical basis of the proposed program? How sound is that theoretical base? (For example, if a mathematics program is based largely on the theories of Piaget, how sound do those theories appear in the light of current research?)

2. What is the nature of the research done to document the validity of the proposed program? What is the quantity and quality of the research done in actual classroom settings? (For example, if you are considering the adoption of a mathematics program, determine how many studies have been done using the program and what types of students and schools were included in the studies' samples.)

3. Is there evidence of large-scale implementation in the program evaluation? If so, what comparisons were made with traditional programs? How realistic was the evaluation? What was the duration? What was the setting? (p. 249)

Although you may feel unprepared and inadequate when it comes to judging experimental and quasi-experimental research and its validity and applicability to instruction and programs in your school, you will gain expertise with practice. Use these simple guidelines to help you become a better consumer of research.

*Internal validity* can be claimed for a study in which there are few if any other reasonable explanations for the results other than the effect of the treatment. If one can think of several plausible explanations for the results in addition to the treatment, the study lacks internal validity. Controlling for alternative explanations (i.e., making sure they are accounted for) is essential to obtaining internal validity. Another way to ensure internal validity is to use random assignment—participants are randomly assigned to both the treatment group and the control group.

*External validity* means that the results of a particular piece of research can be generalized to other groups. "The people [students] involved directly, the sample, are only of interest to the extent to which they inform us about similar groups of people not directly involved in the study" (Smith & Glass, 1987, p. 6). If a group of third-graders in Tokyo, Japan, learn mathematics in a certain way, would the methodology have the same effect on your third-grade students?

*Replication* is the duplication of an earlier study that confirms the previous findings. The replication uses an identical treatment but with a different group of subjects. The replicability of a research study refers to the way in which the methodology and treatment conditions were described so as to make it possible for the study to be replicated. "This description should extend to the characteristics of the setting, tasks, service deliverers, and procedures and operations of the study itself" (Smith & Glass, 1987, p. 153).

*Convergence* means that the findings of many different studies done by different researchers and employing different research methodologies (e.g., quantitative and ethnographic) converge around one conclusion. Only when convergence begins to occur should educators consider implementing a program or methodology on a large scale.

*Logical validity* is probably one of the easier indicators to evaluate. Does the whole thing hang together? Can you follow the argument and figure out if the research supported the hypothesis?

*Construct validity* refers to how well the researchers have defined and measured a characteristic or trait under study. If the research involves problem-solving ability, for example, is the test the researchers used to measure a student's ability to solve problems a valid measure of that ability? Has it been standardized? Is it described in the *Mental Measurements Yearbook,* for example?

*Size* tells you the scale of the study. A large-scale study should involve the assignment of thousands of subjects in a variety of locations to a variety of treatments. Examples of large-scale studies include the 1997 TIMSS, an investigation of mathematics achievement around the world, and Project Follow-Through, an investigation of nine different early childhood models of instruction from 1967 to 1995 (Bock, Stebbins, & Proper, 1977).

*Controls* are statistical methods used by the researcher to rule out and eliminate variables other than the one under examination. For example, when comparing student achievement in two schools, a researcher must control for SES (socioeconomic status), a variable known for its correlation with achievement. Controlling for this variable allows the researcher to compare achievement without the static created by other variables. The Tennessee Value-Added Assessment System (TVAAS), for example, allows researchers to factor out SES when assessing the gains made by students over a three-year period. TVAAS reports allow school systems to pinpoint grade or curriculum problems and successes and to direct efforts and resources accordingly. "School reports, for example, may inform principals not only about how effective the fourth-grade math program is in regard to enhancing student academic gains but also whether it is equally effective in encouraging such growth in both its high-achieving and low-achieving students and whether all teachers are achieving similar results" (Sanders, Saxton, & Horn, 1997, p. 136).

*Peer-reviewed journals* help you consider where the article or research study has been published. A peer-reviewed scholarly journal is the most trustworthy place of publication. "Peer review typically entails blind review of a manuscript by a panel of experts selected by an editor. Panelists are not given the author's name, and the author is not given the reviewers' names. All criticisms and replies are exchanged through the editor" (Stone & Clements, 1998, p. 12). *Review of Educational Research, Journal of*

*Applied Behavioral Analysis, American Educational Research Journal,* and *American Journal of Education* are just a few of such journals.

## Qualitative Research

The second major category of education research is qualitative in nature. This type of research relies on observation and written description rather than objective measurement. The researcher deals primarily in words and pictures rather than numbers and statistics. Qualitative research consists of the subjective observations of one individual who becomes part of a setting or culture over an extended period of time. The ideal qualitative researcher brings few preconceived notions to the experience but seeks to record and describe. "Quality is the essential character or nature of something; quantity is the amount. Quality is the what; quantity is the how much. Qualitative refers to the meaning, the definition or analogy or model or metaphor characterizing something, while quantitative assumes the meaning and refers to the measure of it" (Dabbs, 1982, p. 32).

## Indicators of Quality Qualitative Research

While qualitative research does not lend itself to the same type of evaluation as quantitative research, there are eight indicators that point to outstanding qualitative studies. Quantitative research is much easier to evaluate because the criteria are objective; a study either has internal and external validity or it doesn't. The research either follows the rules that govern this type of research or it doesn't. But when evaluating qualitative research, one is more directly critiquing the author, and questioning a qualitative researcher's personal experiences or conclusions can often seem as if one is attacking the researcher's personal credibility.

*Adequate time spent in collecting data.* Did the researcher spend enough time "on location" to collect a sufficient amount of data? For example, spending a few afternoons working with a small group of third-graders is not enough time to draw any valid conclusions about how students learn math. Graduate students in cultural anthropology at many universities are expected to spend at least one full year observing and documenting before writing their dissertations.

*Logical validity.* Does the researcher offer logical and sensible conclusions? Does the researcher convince you that the conclusions are valid?

*Adequate access to data.* Did the researcher form substantial enough relationships with the subjects of the study to gain their confidence and credibility?

*Detailed and precise descriptions.* Does the researcher provide you with a rich, varied, and deep understanding of the setting and the people studied? A quality ethnographic study contains an overabundance of description, enough for readers not only to read it for their own purposes but also to read it to understand the purposes of the study. In *Japanese Lessons: A Year in a Japanese School Through the Eyes of an American Anthropologist and Her Children,* Gail Benjamin (1997) gives the reader a unique view of the Japanese educational system and also shows us which aspects of that system would be difficult to implement in the United States.

*Naturalness of the data.* Does the researcher's personality play a secondary role to the descriptions?

*Significance.* Does the study address important questions, and are those questions answered adequately? Makoto Yoshida's 1999 ethnographic study of the Japanese lesson-study process offers us a rare glimpse into how teachers meticulously plan lessons, observe and critique the teaching of these lessons, and continue to hone them to perfection. The study also details the problems, conflicts, and deeper issues that are involved in this complex process.

*Self-Evaluation.* Are the researcher's preconceptions and biases explicitly communicated, and were steps taken to control for these in the study? Teachers who conduct qualitative research in their own classroom may learn a great deal to inform their own teaching practices but may be too personally involved to conduct an ethnographic study with any implications for further practice.

*Confirmation.* Has the researcher checked the conclusions with other sources and observers? (Smith & Glass, 1987, p. 278).

When it comes to high-quality research, more is better. A single study showing a relationship between two variables is never as convincing as a substantial body of literature all pointing in the same direction. There are two types of studies that compile and summarize research focused on a specific topic or program: literature reviews and meta-analyses.

*The Power of Size*

## Literature Reviews

Literature reviews are summaries of a body of research relative to a certain topic or question. The author of a review assembles all of the pertinent studies (e.g., all of the research done regarding the errors students typically make when learning how to add and subtract two-digit numbers), reads and assimilates them, then draws conclusions for the reader based on that entire body of research. The quality of the conclusions in a review of the literature is only as reliable as (1) the quality of the individual studies used to draw the conclusions and (2) the expertise of the individual drawing the conclusions. While literature reviews can be helpful as a means of determining what's out there on a given topic, the reader must always be wary of the biases of the interpreter and the quality of what is being interpreted. Jackson (1976) evaluated 36 literature reviews from journals in education, psychology, and sociology and found the following problems:

► Reviewers didn't bother to look at earlier reviews of the literature on the topic and just drew their own conclusions.

► Reviewers often focused their discussion on a small portion of the studies they reviewed.

► Reviewers misled the readers and misrepresented the studies.

▶ Reviewers failed to assess possible relationships between the characteristics of the studies and the study findings.

▶ Reviewers reported very little about their own methods of reviewing to permit the reader to judge the validity of their conclusions.

## Meta-Analyses

Meta-analyses are statistical analyses of the findings of many different studies on a single topic. This approach to synthesizing the findings of many research studies eliminates many of the problems inherent in the literature review (Glass & McGaw, 1981).

*Fact or Fancy?*

## Opinion and Theory Building

Opinion and theory-building articles are thoughtful, serious essays in which the author either offers commentary on an existing body of research or advances new ways in which to examine or interpret the study of a topic. An article by von Glaserfeld and Steffe (1991), for example, suggests the use of conceptual models to help educational scientists who develop theories of mathematics learning test their theories in the arena of educational practice. The article is thought provoking and instructive, but it is *not* research, and the authors do not claim that it is.

## Follow the Citations

One cannot always assume that the source citations (e.g., "Doe, 1997, p. 15") found in an article refer to actual research. They may well be opinions or articles that merely describe or confirm the problem. You won't know until you head off to the Internet or the library to read them yourself. For example, the von Glaserfeld and Steffe article mentioned previously has been cited as an example of research supporting the efficacy of a certain instructional approach (Battista, 1999 [On-line]), when, in reality, it merely suggests the need for researchers and educators to use a common language as they examine how students learn mathematics. "Many influential recommendations for teaching practice are really academic musings, devoid of any real research base—a fact that too many practitioners only find out the hard way: in the classroom" (Grossen, 1996, p. 8).

*Where's the Research?*

A well-known fast food chain popularized a commercial some years ago in which a feisty senior citizen was shown inspecting a competitor's hamburger and whining, "Where's the beef?" After reading this chapter, you are certainly justified in paraphrasing that question as it applies to mathematics instruction: "Where's the research?"

The California State Board of Education asked that very question and contracted with five individuals (Dixon, Carnine, Lee, Wallin, & Chard, 1998a) to locate high-quality *experimental* research in mathematics, evaluate it according to well-established principles of experimental design (i.e., the ones mentioned earlier), and synthesize the findings. The California Board of Education wanted to use the review to inform their decisions about mathematics standards and textbook adoptions. The team used a meticulous process. From a total of 8,727 published studies of mathematics in elementary and secondary schools, they identified only 956 articles that satisfied the minimum identification criteria of being an experimental study of mathematics. The remaining studies failed to satisfy the criteria of high-quality experimental research. The evaluators then used the evaluative criteria for experimental research cited earlier to determine "if an instructional approach was effective when evaluated using scientifically valid research methods, and to determine under what conditions and for which students the approach produced positive effects on criterial measures" (Dixon et al., 1998a, p. 8). Only 231 of the original 956 studies made it through an initial screening of construct, internal, and external validity. When the methodologies of those 231 studies were screened for internal and external validity, only 110 studies were deemed to be of high quality. The final report titled *Review of High Quality Experimental Mathematics Research* is very instructive, not only for the approach it used in evaluating such a large body of research, but for the summary of its findings and how they speak to mathematics instruction in your school. Many of the studies will be reviewed in Chapter 4 as we examine how you can make research-based changes in your school to increase mathematics achievement.

There is much work to be done, however. We need far more high quality research than we currently have to inform mathematics instruction. In *Every Child Mathematically Proficient: An Action Plan* (1998), produced by the Learning First Alliance, which is made up of organizations representing teacher educators, teachers, administrators, parents, and school board members, the authors summarize the current state of mathematics research thusly: "Reliance on both tradition and educational fads has played too big a role in mathematics education. There must, of course, be a place for the investigation of new ideas, since the fields of mathematics and cognitive science are dynamic and continually yield new knowledge that may have implications for mathematics teaching and learning. Large-scale practice, however, should not be based on the publication of a new research paper or a current enthusiasm, but should occur when a body of sound research convinces us that a change will lead to better student achievement" (p. 19).

# The Alterable Variables

*"If achievement scores cannot be related to educational factors that can be changed (that is, cannot be related to making better educational choices), there seems little point in going through the massive efforts needed to gather cross-national information."*

—Schmidt et al., 1999, p. 113

*"Achievement consists of never giving up. . . . If there is no dark and dogged will, there will be no shining accomplishment; if there is no dull and determined effort, there will be no brilliant achievement." —Hsun Tzu*

—Watson, 1967, p. 18

f you want to raise mathematics achievement, be ready to deal with both bad news and good news. First, the bad news: The variables that influence student achievement are multiple and complex. Many of the most powerful ones are completely out of the control of educators, such as the socioeconomic status of the neighborhood, the educational level of parents, students' readiness to learn, and students' cognitive abilities. When confronted with studies that strongly associate student achievement with these immutables (Coleman, 1966), it is all too easy for educators to become demoralized. When one reads about "First in the World," the consortium of schools in the well-heeled northern suburbs of Chicago whose fourth- and eighth-grade students' TIMSS scores in both mathematics and science were comparable to the top-performing schools around the world, it is easy to be cynical (Hawkes, Kimmelman, & Kroeze, 1997, pp. 30–33). After all, how many districts can afford to spend $9,821 per pupil? How many schools that are battling low mathematics achievement can claim the following demographics: fewer than 2% of students on free and reduced lunch and a mobility rate of just under 4%? (Illinois School Report Card, 1998).

Don't be discouraged, however. There is also good news. You do have control over a great deal. The power is there; you just need to tap into it. There are half a dozen variables that can be altered in research-based ways to directly influence mathematics achievement. There are also many environmental variables (e.g., teacher morale, student discipline, and parent-teacher communication) that if changed could have an impact not only on mathematics achievement, but also on achievement in every subject area.

So forget about what is beyond your control and concentrate instead on what you can control. Harnessing the energy, creativity, and collective wisdom of your faculty, examine the following list of alterable variables to determine which ones might need to be addressed in your school.

1. Change the content—what you believe is most critical in mathematics for students to know and be able to do.

2. Change how you connect the content—the coordination and articulation of the mathematics content throughout your school.

3. Change the materials you use to teach mathematics—the textbooks.

4. Change how you teach mathematics—instructional methodologies.

5. Change your expectations for how much of the content every student can learn.

6. Change how you assess student mastery of the content.

> "One wag has argued that it's easier to move a cemetery than to delete a topic from the school curriculum."
> —Leinwand, 1994 [On-line].

The sections that follow describe each of these six variables and offer possible ways in which you might alter the variable to influence mathematics achievement.

## Change the Content

One possible way to raise mathematics achievement is to change the content to focus on what you believe is most critical in mathematics for students to know and be able to do. The what of learning can be defined and studied in multiple ways. If your personal academic background in mathematics is rusty or nonexistent, consult others. Be sure to include in your survey the opinions of seasoned professors of pure and applied mathematics, those who employ mathematics in their careers, and math educators. My recommendations based on such a survey can be found in Chapter 5. Although the term *standards* is used popularly to encompass the content of learning, for the purposes of our discussion we will use the term *curriculum* to refer to the content of learning. Most educators have some kind of working definition of curriculum in their toolkit, but to *which* curriculum does the definition refer? Fenwick English (1992) enumerates several:

1. The *formal curriculum,* that which usually appears in curriculum guides, state regulations, or officially sanctioned scope and sequence charts

2. The *informal curriculum,* the unrecognized and unofficial aspects of design-ing or delivering curriculum, such as the values that are at work in making the selection of what is taught

3. The *hidden curriculum,* the conventions and unspoken lessons that teachers teach every day, such as showing respect, doing your work on time, and so forth

4. The *written curriculum,* that which is actually contained in a binder or writ-ten in an official document

5. The *taught curriculum,* that which the teacher actually spends time teaching in the classroom

6. The *tested curriculum,* that which is included on the test that is given, be it a state-developed standardized assessment or a curriculum-based assessment (pp. 7–9)

The TIMSS researchers who studied mathematics and science curricula around the world developed a slightly different model to explain the content of learning. They described four curricula:

1. The *intended curriculum,* the standards or "intentions, aims, goals"

2. The *potentially implemented curriculum,* the textbooks

3. The *implemented curriculum,* that which is taught in the classroom through a variety of "strategies, practices, and activities"

4. The *attained curriculum,* the skills and knowledge students actually dem-onstrate on tests (Schmidt et al., 1996, pp. 17, 30)

Labaree (1999) suggests still another model for organizing the variety of curric-ula with which educators have to deal:

1. The *rhetorical curriculum,* ideas put forward by educational leaders, policy makers, and professors about what curriculum should be, as embodied in re-ports, speeches, and college texts

2. The *formal curriculum,* written curriculum policies put in place by school dis-tricts and embodied in curriculum guides and textbooks

3. The *curriculum in use,* the content that teachers actually teach in individual classrooms

4. The *received curriculum,* the content that students actually learn in these classrooms (p. 42)

What constitutes the mathematics curriculum in your school? The state stan-dards? A curriculum guide produced by a district committee? A set of school out-comes? Or is the curriculum whatever topics or chapters of a textbook an individual teacher decides to cover?

Determining the curriculum is the first essential activity of schooling. "Curricu-lum is something concrete—something that can be pointed to—something that a teacher can implement and something that can be evaluated to see if its goals have been accomplished" (Snyder, Bolin, & Zumwalt, 1992, p. 427).

Curriculum refers not only to the actual content but also to its scope (how much students are expected to learn in a given grade level or course) and sequence (what topics or courses are taught first, second, etc.). Choosing curriculum and defining standards can be contentious processes, however, because "standards, ultimately, are statements about what is most valued" (Hiebert, 1999, p. 2). So don't expect that changing what you choose to teach will be an easy process. Parents, teachers, and even students have opinions about what is important; every school, district, and state has its own opinion about what should be taught. In the United States, we value diversity, and we prize local control.

The curricula of mathematics in various countries around the world have been well documented and studied as part of the TIMSS study (Schmidt et al., 1997). As one considers the lower mathematics achievement of U.S. students in comparison to their international peers, this question invariably arises: How do the curricula of those countries differ from the United States? Since we do not have a national curricula as such, the investigators developed what they called a composite curriculum, "the aggregate policies, intentions, and goals of the many educational subsystems making up the loose U.S. federation of guiding educational visions in mathematics" (Schmidt et al., 1997a, p. 13).

Here is what the observers learned about the mathematics curriculum in the United States:

▶ We keep adding new topics and approaches without abandoning other content topics. Teachers end up choosing the things they want to teach based on personal preference because they know they cannot possibly cover everything in the curriculum. Consequently, every student is exposed to a slightly different version of mathematics than his grade-level peers in other classrooms, schools, districts, and states.

▶ We cover many topics in each grade and do not focus on mastering a few strategic topics. Our curriculum is so broad that teachers must rush in order to cover the material; hence, students do not have the time needed for in-depth study and mastery.

▶ We keep the same topics in the curriculum for years, sometimes through six or seven grade levels, so there is no sense of urgency to bring a student to mastery in a specific area. Teachers take comfort in knowing that students will be exposed to the same topics again the next year, and the next, and the next.

In summary, "these curricula [in reference to U.S. documents] express an intention to do something of everything and, on average, less of any one thing. The general impact of these unfocused curricula in mathematics and science likely includes lower yields from mathematics and science education in the U.S." (Schmidt et al., 1997a, p. 51).

What are the practical applications of this information for you and your staff? Take a closer look at the curriculum you expect your students to learn, whether it be spelled out in the form of state standards, district level learning outcomes, or just a list of topics that teachers in your school have compiled. Is it a mile wide and an inch deep? If you have an unfocused approach similar to that described in the TIMSS report, it is undoubtedly contributing to depressed mathematics achievement in your school. Are teachers in different grade levels covering the same topics year after year, never worrying about mastery because they know the same topic will be covered again? Do they rush from topic to topic desperately trying to cover everything without doing an adequate job of bringing students to mastery of anything?

In our schoolwide effort to raise mathematics achievement at the elementary school where I served as principal, we determined that most teachers in second through sixth grades spent a month or more reviewing previously taught and often mastered topics, leaving less time for new and more challenging material. This practice resulted in sixth-grade graduates who had covered basic skills ad nauseum but had never spent time on problem solving, geometry, measurement, and statistics. "No problem. I'll get it again next year." Sixth-grade teachers, although they would never confess to it, secretly counted on the seventh-grade remedial math class to make up for their students' deficiencies. This mindset effectively ensured that a large percentage of our students would never acquire the math skills needed to succeed in algebra, thus consigning them to innumeracy. If you want to raise mathematics achievement, define in terms that teachers can understand what you expect students to know and be able to do. (Chapter 5 focuses in detail on the essential learnings of mathematics in kindergarten through Grade 12.)

Defining desired outcomes for students is only the first step, however. Having the objectives in writing does not guarantee the content will be taught by teachers or mastered by students. The expectations need to get into the lifeblood of the school, into the taught curriculum, and, most particularly, into the mastered and tested curriculum. The content must be talked about, argued about, then agreed upon by teachers across as well as up and down the grade levels. Teachers need to be continually focused on bringing students to mastery of the content. This brings us to a second powerful alterable variable: the connections of the content in your school.

## Change How You Connect the Content

Changing how you connect the content—the coordination and articulation of the mathematics content throughout your school—is a second possible way to influence mathematics achievement. A principal recently consulted with me regarding raising achievement in his school. I asked, *"What is being taught in the first grades of your school, and how is it being taught?"* He hesitated for a moment and then confessed with some chagrin that there were eight different answers to that question—one for each of his eight sections of first grade. When one computes the possible combinations and permutations of the various curricula (i.e., written, hidden, taught, tested), then multiplies that number times eight class sections, one can immediately see a major problem—lack of coordination and articulation. Coordination is the lateral or horizontal focus and connectivity of curriculum in a school environment. A bird's-eye view of all of the first-grade classes might reveal a lack of common focus and connectivity. Once you have agreed upon the curriculum (what you expect students to know and be able to do), the next step is to call a grade-level meeting (in this case, the first grade) to discuss how the teachers might standardize their instruction to meet these outcomes. Teachers pride themselves on their creativity, the unique units they create, the materials they develop, and the projects they do in their classrooms. If these activities are producing the agreed-upon outcomes, lack of standardization is not a major concern.

If they are not, what your teachers are currently doing must be replaced with instruction that gets results.

Coordination between all of the sections at a grade level is only the beginning. Articulation from one grade level to the next is also critical. "When a curriculum is articulated, it is focused and connected vertically from one grade to the next or [in a district] from one school to the next" (English, 1992, p. 18). Imagine the confusion that takes place each fall when eight sections of first grade are reconfigured into eight second-grade classrooms. Each second-grade teacher could well be faced with eight unique groups of students, each having completed first grade with a different attained curriculum. Then the second-grade teachers do their own thing and a chaotic curricular spiral spins out of control. By the time the original cohort of first-graders graduates to middle school, the odds against any 10 students being able to know and do the same things are astronomical.

Durkin and Shire (1991) describe just one area in which the lack of coordination and articulation can cause poor performance and student anxiety in mathematics—lexical ambiguity (p. 72). Mathematics has more than its share of ambiguous words. For students whose language development and reading skills are below grade level, words that are spelled the same but have different meanings (leaves as outgrowths of trees or leaves as used in the process of subtraction) and words that have different but related meanings (product as something that is made and product as a quantity obtained by multiplication) pose serious problems. When the teacher begins to attach symbols to different words in different contexts, confusion reigns supreme. Consider the different words used for the equal sign (=): equals, means, makes, leaves, the same as, gives, and results in. And any one of these words in itself has multiple meanings.

The difficulties that many children encounter with lexical ambiguities are compounded when teachers also use their own set of terms and explanations for algorithms and problem-solving strategies. The need for more scripted lessons and standardization in mathematics instruction is imperative, especially when working with at-risk students.

Think about the benefits for our eight classes of first-grade students if their teachers could collectively agree on a common mathematics vocabulary that would then be used by the teachers in the second, third, and following grades. Lexical ambiguity problems as well as other coordination and articulation problems can be diminished or even eliminated when all teachers use the same textbooks and/or work from a set of standardized lesson plans. Unfortunately, when teachers function as mere guides on the side and students are encouraged to construct their own mathematical meaning, results vary widely from classroom to classroom. Strong instructional leadership is needed to bring a measure of standardization to instructional materials, methods, and outcomes.

> "The reformers who provide teachers with theories—but no evidence that they are effective and no details for how to use them—are really demanding that teachers do most of the work for them. To ask that teachers create all of their own tools and curricula is like asking doctors to invent all of their own drugs; like asking airline pilots to build their own airplanes. When would teachers have time to do this? Engineering a highly effective instruction sequence would more than consume most teachers' private time."
> —Grossen, 1996, p. 27

## Change the Textbooks

Changing the textbooks you use to teach mathematics is a third possible way to notch up achievement. Textbooks are undoubtedly more influential than curriculum guides or standards' documents in dictating instruction. "While teachers may select from or supplement textbooks, for many U.S. mathematics and science teachers, textbooks at a 'micro' level are the curriculum that guides mathematics and science instruction" (Schmidt et al., 1997a, p. 53).

Unfortunately, the mathematics textbooks used in the United States reflect the same deficiencies in focus as our curriculum. Here is what the TIMSS researchers found.

◆ U.S. textbooks at fourth, eighth, and twelfth grade contain remarkably large numbers of mathematics topics. "For example, Japan has 20 topics in fourth grade while in the United States, fourth-grade textbooks typically contain 30 to 35 topics. At eighth grade Japanese students are expected to master 10 topics while in the United States the textbooks still include an average of 30 to 35 topics" (Schmidt et al., 1997a, p. 54).

◆ Not only do our textbooks weigh more and contain more topics, they contain fewer sequences of extended attention to the more important topics. "Among the fourth-grade mathematics textbooks investigated, the five topics receiving the most textbook space accounted on average for about 60 percent of space in the U.S. textbooks but govern 85 percent of textbook space internationally" (Schmidt et al., 1997a, p. 57). Not only do U.S. students cover more topics, but they are expected to master them with less focused instruction.

◆ Textbooks in the United States tend to present far easier problems than do comparable textbooks in other countries. Even when complex problems are presented in U.S. textbooks, they are not presented frequently enough to allow our children to become skilled at solving such problems (Geary, 1994, p. 96). A third-grade mathematics textbook that has been translated into English from Russian, for example, consists of nothing but problems (Pcholko, Bantova, Moro, & Pyshkalo, 1978/1992). Most of the more than 1,000 problems are of the variety we commonly call *story problems*. How would your third-grade students or teachers respond to problems similar to these?

> "10 railroad cars carrying coal arrived at a station at 8 a.m. After 15 minutes, a youth brigade began unloading the cars, each car taking an average of 12 minutes to unload. At what time was the unloading of the railroad cars completed?"
> (Pcholko et al., 1978, p. 109).

> "On the moon all objects are 6 times lighter than on Earth. What was the weight on the moon of Kunokhod-1 [the Moonwalker space vehicle], which weighed 756 kg. on Earth? of Lunokhod-2, which weighed 840 kg on Earth? of a man who weighs 72 kg on Earth?"
> (Pcholko et al., 1978, p. 117).

Given the spectrum of mathematics textbooks available for purchase in the United States, choosing the best is a high priority. A comparison of how textbooks in Japan teach mathematical problem solving versus those used in the United States points out some startling differences (Mayer, Sims, & Tajika, 1995). Figure 4.1 summarizes the results of the comparison.

The reader quickly realizes that "cognitive modeling of problem-solving processes is emphasized more in Japan than in the United States, whereas drill and practice on the product of problem solving is emphasized more in the United States than in Japan. Japanese textbooks seem to assume the learner is a cognitively active problem

**FIGURE 4.1.**
A Comparison of How Textbooks Teach Problem Solving

| Research Findings | Textbook Characteristics | Japanese Texts Have | American Texts Have |
|---|---|---|---|
| Meaningful explanation is critical for promoting problem-solving abilities (Mayer, 1987). | Length/quality of instructional explanation | Longer explanations | Shorter explanations |
| Importance of worked-out examples and concrete analogies for promoting problem-solving skills (Mayer, 1987). | Presence of worked-out examples and concrete analogies | More worked-out examples | Fewer worked-out examples |
| Certain kinds of illustrations have more instructional value than others. Highly interesting but irrelevant material diminishes student recall of important information (Levin & Mayer, 1993). | Relevant as opposed to decorative, irrelevant illustrations | More relevant illustrations | More irrelevant illustrations |
| Successful programs rely on the use of cognitive modeling techniques such as detailed descriptions of worked-out examples (Mayer, 1992). | Presence of worked out examples of problem-solving | More worked-out problem-solving examples | Fewer worked-out problem-solving examples |
| Students build more meaningful connections when presented with multiple representations (Grouws, 1992; Hiebert, 1986). | Presence of symbolic, verbal, and pictorial representations for solving specific problems | More representations for solving problems | Fewer representations for solving problems |
| Students learn more effectively when the topics of the text are organized in a simple and coherent structure (Britton, Woodward, & Binkley, 1993; Jonassen, Beissner, Yacci, 1993). | Organization of text; compactness of text; clear structure; fewer topics covered in more depth | Fewer topics in more depth | More topics in less depth |

Summarized from Mayer, Sims, & Tajika, 1995.

solver who seeks to understand the step-by-step process for solving a class of problems. In contrast, U.S. textbooks seem to assume the learner is a behaviorally active knowledge acquisition machine who learns best from hands-on activity in solving problems with minimal guidance and who needs to be stimulated by interesting decorative illustrations" (Mayer et al., 1995, p. 457).

Consider a popular American middle school/high school mathematics textbook, *Focus on Algebra: An Integrated Approach* (Charles, Thompson, & Garland, 1997). It has become the "poster book" for all that is wrong with mathematics textbooks in the United States. It was first featured in a *Wall Street Journal* column written by Marianne Jennings, a professor at Arizona State University. She encountered the book when her daughter brought it home from her eighth-grade algebra class. Jennings relates her dismay at the contents of the book, noting that it contained "color photos, essays on the Dogon tribe of Africa, and questions such as 'What role should zoos play in today's society?'" Jennings goes on to lament the "Maya Angelou poetry, pictures of Bill Clinton, and little insights from Tabuk and Esteban (youngsters chosen to enlighten students about cultural differences in the ever-fluid concept of slope)" (Jennings, 1996, p. A22).

Martin Gardner, noted math columnist and commentator, had this to say about *Focus on Algebra* in the *New York Review of Books*: "The book's mathematical content is often hard to find in the midst of material that has no clear connection to mathematics. Many pictures have only a slim reference to the text. Magritte's painting of a green apple floating in front of a man's face accompanies some problems about apples. Van Gogh's self-portrait is alongside a problem about the heights and widths of canvases. A picture of the Beatles accompanies a problem about taxes only because of the Beatles' song 'Taxman'" (Gardner, 1998, p. 9–12). This textbook would appear to exemplify many of the problems that characterize American mathematics textbooks.

If changing the textbooks your teachers use to teach mathematics holds great potential for raising achievement, it is also fraught with confusion and controversy. There are four categories of mathematics textbooks at the kindergarten through Grade 8 levels currently available for purchase:

1. Well-known and popular mathematics basal series published by major textbook houses (e.g., McGraw-Hill and Scott Foresman/Addison Wesley)

2. Math series developed specifically in response to the NCTM 1989 Standards document, some funded by the National Science Foundation (e.g., *Everyday Mathematics* from the University of Chicago School Mathematics Project) and others developed by smaller publishing houses (e.g., *Mathland* from Creative Publications)

3. Textbooks/series published by small publishing houses that are strongly focused on content and do not feature approaches such as cooperative learning or student-centered discovery (e.g., *Saxon Math* and *Connecting Math Concepts,* a direct instruction mathematics program published by McGraw-Hill)

4. Foreign texts published in English (Curriculum Planning & Development Division, Ministry of Education, Singapore, 1999) or translated into English (University of Chicago School Mathematics Project Translations)

Figure 4.2 summarizes these four categories.

There are several important considerations in evaluating textbooks for use in your school, but foremost among them is getting the best possible match between the contents/topics of the textbook and your curriculum (learning standards). Figure 4.3, Textbook Evaluation Questionnaire, includes a broad range of questions designed to help you evaluate any textbook/series from a variety of perspectives.

**FIGURE 4.2.**
Comparison of Mathematics Textbooks

| Types of Textbooks | Possible Concerns in the Selection Process* |
|---|---|
| 1. Major Publishers | 1. Inclusive, very comprehensive textbooks containing both traditional and standards-based instructional approaches |
| | 2. Teacher guides that often fail to prioritize, leaving important instructional decisions to teachers |
| | 3. Increased odds of great variability in what is taught in classrooms, as teachers select the skills and approaches with which they feel comfortable |
| | 4. Wide variety of supplementary materials, which makes it difficult for teachers to determine what is of highest priority |
| | 5. Mile-wide, inch-deep coverage of math topics in some cases |
| | 6. Large quantities of colorful illustrations and irrelevant activities; highly distractible students and teachers may find it difficult to stay on the task of mastering math objectives |
| 2. NCTM-Based/NSF Sponsored Programs | 1. No emphasis on memorization, computation, or mastery of algorithms |
| | 2. Teacher as co-learner rather than dispenser of knowledge |
| | 3. In some cases there are no textbooks, only blackline masters; teachers may have to spend a great deal of preparation time in copying the masters, gathering manipulative materials, distributing materials, and so on |
| NCTM-Based/ Independent Publishers | 4. Teachers will need extensive training in cooperative learning techniques and in "facilitating" instruction, rather than in "teaching" |
| | 5. Parents will need extensive preparation for the lack of traditional homework assignments, lack of memorization or mastery of traditional algorithms, and lack of a textbook; they will have many doubts about the program's philosophy and may well mount a campaign against the adoption of the textbook |
| 3. Non-NCTM Based Publishers | 1. Lack of supplementary materials and colorful textbooks—teachers often "judge a book by its cover" and cannot judge instructional merits apart from the traditional textbook trappings |
| | 2. Lack of in-service training and support |
| | 3. Carefully scripted lessons that some teachers may find objectionable |
| 4. Foreign Texts | 1. Teacher guides assume a highly knowledgeable and competent teaching staff |
| | 2. Examples and vocabulary contain metric measurements and country-specific terms. |

*Every concern does not apply to every program. This chart is not intended to take the place of a thorough examination and evaluation of the textbooks under consideration by a broad-based committee.
NCTM = National Council of Teachers of Mathematics; NSF = National Science Foundation

**FIGURE 4.3.**
Textbook Evaluation Questionnaire

### Structure of the Program

1. How many school days are needed to adequately teach all the important lessons?
2. Does the program present a few basic topics in depth, organized into coherent lessons, rather than an overwhelming collective of fragments?
3. Does the manual give comprehensive teacher's guidance?
4. Are the instructions for teachers clear as to scheduling and presentation of individual lessons?
5. Do the instructions for teachers include clear statements of the lesson objectives to be made by the teacher at the beginning and/or conclusion of the lesson?
6. Are the lesson presentations well designed and field tested?
7. Are prerequisite skills thoroughly taught with enough guided practice to ensure student success before introducing new material?
8. Do students receive adequate practice in memorizing basic facts before they encounter them in problem exercises?
9. Are the lesson presentations scripted or at least detailed enough to assist novices?
10. Does the program contain an assessment component?
11. If the program contains many supplemental materials/activities, is there assistance for teachers with prioritizing which ones are essential and which are "nice but not necessary"?
12. Does the program contain an overabundance of nonmathematical themes, distracting illustrations, extraneous examples, and unfocused small-group activities?

### Topic Coverage

1. Are the topics contained in the school's/district's curriculum/standards/student outcomes also included in the textbook? Are they included in sufficient depth for student mastery?
2. Which topics are targeted for mastery? Which are targeted for exposure?
3. Are the topics arranged so that the prerequisites needed to understand new material have been covered?
4. Does the presentation sequence explicate topics in a logical manner?
5. Are teacher time and student time both used wisely?
6. What is the program's philosophy with regard to mental arithmetic, algorithms, and calculators?
7. Are students expected to master the algorithms (addition, subtraction, multiplication, and division)? At what grade levels are they expected to achieve mastery?
8. Are students expected/required to develop other strategies even if they already know the standard algorithm?
9. Does the program develop automaticity in computational skills as well as strong problem-solving abilities?
10. Do upper-grade texts support the goal of algebra for all students by ninth grade, and algebra for a large percentage of students by eighth grade (i.e., inclusion of algebraic skills and concepts)?

**FIGURE 4.3.** Continued

## Mathematical Depth

1. Is the coverage sufficient to prepare students for the next level of mathematics?
2. Is the coverage sufficient to prepare students for solving appropriate real-world applications?
3. Is the level of difficulty such that students will be well prepared for the next level of mathematics?
4. What is the amount of repeating material from earlier grades?
5. Are specific topics taught with the expectation that they will be mastered at that grade level?
6. Is there sufficient review to facilitate retention?
7. Are explanations and examples well written?
8. Is there a glossary available for definition of terms?

## Emphasis on Problem Solving

1. Are lessons embedded within a familiar situational context so that verbal, visual, and symbolic representations are interconnected?
2. Is there an abundance of worked-out examples (i.e., problems in which all of the work is shown as well as the answer) to emphasize the process of problem solving?
3. Are students presented with a verbal-written statement of the solution rule after familiar worked-out examples have been presented?
4. Do the problem sets include a mix of current and previous types of problems?
5. Are a sufficient number of problem-solving examples presented to enable students to master new skills?

## Quality and Sufficiency of Student Work

1. Does the program support high achievement levels? Is there sufficient "academic press"?
2. Is the quantity of student work sufficient to permit mastery by most students?
3. Does student practice work contain more difficult problems?
4. Do the students consistently work on a variety of problems so that practice on any single content area is distributed over many days?
5. Are homework worksheets clear enough that parents can assist students as needed?
6. Is practice emphasized?

These evaluation questions were developed using the following resources:
1. Clopton, McKeown, McKeown, & Clopton (1999)
2. Schmidt et. al. (1997a)
3. American Association for the Advancement of Science (1999)
4. Mayer et al. (1995, Summer)
5. Stein, Silbert, & Carnine (1997)

What do you want students to know and be able to do when they leave a specific grade level or course in your school? Without a set of standards (outcomes) to guide your textbook selection process, you might as well weigh the books and choose the heaviest or calculate which company offers the most freebies. If you choose a textbook based *solely* on the NCTM Standards, you will probably choose one type of text. If you choose a textbook based on the standards of the states of California, Texas, or Virginia, you will undoubtedly choose another. Choosing textbooks can often be a highly controversial activity (Colvin, 1999b, p. A3).

In October 1999, the U.S. Department of Education endorsed 10 mathematics programs for kindergarten through 12th grade, describing them as "exemplary" or "promising." The exemplary programs are Cognitive Tutor Algebra, College Preparatory Mathematics (CPM), Connected Mathematics Program (CMP), Core-Plus Mathematics Project, and Interactive Mathematics Program (IMP). The "promising programs" are Everyday Mathematics, MathLand, Middle School Mathematics Through Applications Project (MMAP), Number Power, and the University of Chicago School Mathematics Project (UCSMP).

Shortly thereafter, a group of nearly 200 mathematicians and scientists, including several Nobel Laureates and other eminent scholars, urged the Department of Education to withdraw their endorsement. In a letter sent to Secretary of Education Richard Riley (open letter, 1999 [Online]) and reprinted in a full page advertisement in the November 18, 1999, *Washington Post* (p. A5), the group asked that school districts not take the words *exemplary* and *promising* in their dictionary meanings and that they exercise caution in choosing mathematics programs. They further called upon Secretary Riley to "withdraw the entire list of mathematics curricula, for further consideration, and to announce that withdrawal to the public."

When you are evaluating mathematics textbooks, read as widely as you can and consider as many viewpoints as possible. Here are some summaries that evaluate mathematics textbooks using the 1989 NCTM Standards as a benchmark:

1. *Middle Grades Mathematics Textbooks: A Benchmarks-Based Evaluation* is a publication of the American Association for the Advancement of Science (1999 [On-line]). Thirteen textbook series appropriate for middle schools are evaluated. The summary reports point out weaknesses where supplementary materials and teaching may be needed.

2. *Curriculum Summaries* is a project of the K–12 Mathematics Curriculum Center, which is funded by the National Science Foundation. The Center was established in 1997 by Education Development Center, Inc., Newton, Massachusetts. *Curriculum Summaries* (1999 [On-line]) contains information about the 13 programs that were developed specifically to address the recommendations of the 1989 NCTM Standards.

3. *Choosing a Standards-Based Mathematics Curriculum* was originally developed by the aforementioned Education Development Center. The document, now available commercially, sets forth a process that districts can use in adopting a new mathematics curriculum. Although the guide focuses on the 13 curricula evaluated in the *Curriculum Summaries*, the ideas are not specific to these programs.

4. *Exemplary & Promising Mathematics Programs* (U.S. Department of Education's Mathematics and Science Expert Panel, 1999 [On-line]) was developed by a panel of mathematics and science experts chosen by the U.S. Department of Education. The report has generated a great deal of controversy, since it endorses programs that are seen by many as lacking in mathematical rigor.

For another perspective, consult mathematics reviews by those who objected to the Education Department's endorsing specific textbooks as exemplary and promising.

The founding members of Mathematically Correct, an activist group made up of professional mathematicians and scientists, give readers another perspective in *Mathematically Correct Algebra I Reviews* (Clopton, McKeown, McKeown, & Clopton, 1998 [On-line]) and *Mathematics Program Reviews for Grades 2, 5, and 7* (Clopton et al., 1999 [On-line]).

In the *American Mathematical Monthly* (1997), Hung-Hsi Wu, a mathematics professor at the University of California at Berkeley, presents for his academic colleagues a thoughtful look at the current mathematics controversy. He sets forth a similar discussion for teachers in the *American Educator* (1999). The articles offer a perspective that is essential to understand before choosing textbooks.

Thus far, we have considered three variables that when altered can influence student achievement: the content, the connections of the content, and the textbooks. But the fourth alterable variable, how you teach, may be the most powerful tool for influencing student achievement. The impact on achievement of comprehensive, coordinated, and articulated curriculum supported by well-written textbooks may be negligible unless it is accompanied by effective teaching from knowledgeable and well-trained teachers.

> "We believe teachers and teaching are the heart of the educational enterprise. . . . . We further believe that a teacher's skill makes a difference in the performance of students, not only in their achievement scores on tests (as important as that might be), but in their sense of fulfillment in school and their feelings of well-being. We do not mean to imply that being skillful substitutes for other human qualities; but we will argue that whatever else teachers do, they perform in the classroom and their actions set the stage for students' experiences—therefore, only a skillful performance will do."
>
> —Saphier & Gower, 1987, p. v

## Change How You Teach

Changing *how* mathematics is taught is far more challenging than merely changing curriculum or textbooks. Changing teachers involves not only getting inside their classrooms, but also tinkering with the complex culture of teaching as it exists in the United States. However, unless teachers change some of the ways they teach, raising mathematics achievement may not be possible.

Just as Kermit the Frog croons, "It's not easy being green," you can lament, "It's not easy being a principal." I agree wholeheartedly. It is a confusing world out there. Here's a perfect example. You've set your goal: raising mathematics achievement. You have a feeling that your teachers as well as the curriculum and the textbooks need to change. You head off to the library to check out some books and encounter a promising title: *Best Practices: New Standards for Teaching and Learning in America's Schools* (Zemelman, Daniels, & Hyde, 1998). The book contains suggestions for reading, writing, mathematics, science, social studies, and the arts; this paperback volume looks like the answer to a principal's prayers. Once you finish raising math achievement you can then move on to the rest of the curriculum.

As you thumb through the pages two statements catch your eye and appear to offer the answers to all of your questions. "In virtually every school subject, we now have recent summary reports, meta-analyses of instructional research, bulletins from pilot classrooms, and landmark sets of professional recommendations. Today there is a strong consensus definition of Best Practice, of state-of-the-art teaching in every critical field" (Zemelman, Daniels & Hyde, 1998, pp. 4–6).

What are these best practices? The authors summarize and organize them into two lists: do less of and do more of.

**The Less List**

Less whole-class directed instruction

Less student passivity—for example, less sitting, listening, and receiving

Less student time reading textbooks

Less attempts by teachers to cover large amounts of material

Less rote memorization of facts and details

Less stress on competition and grades

Less use of and reliance on standardized tests

**The More List**

More experiential, inductive, hands-on learning

More active learning with all the attendant noise of students doing, talking, collaborating

More deep study of a smaller number of topics

More responsibility transferred to students for their work: goal setting, record keeping, monitoring, evaluation

More choice for students—for example, picking their own books

More attention to affective needs and varying cognitive styles of students

More cooperative, collaborative activity

More reliance on descriptive evaluations of student growth

There are few, if any, of the practices on these two lists that the common-sense educator would either reject completely or implement exclusively. There are quite a number of items on the Do-Less-Of List, however, that have substantial empirical research bases to indicate their effectiveness in raising student achievement, for example, direct instruction (Abt, 1976) and student reading of textbooks (Donahue, Voelkl, Campbell, & Mazzeo, 1999), particularly among children who are at risk of academic failure. And there are items on the Do-More-Of List that have little, if any, research support (e.g., attention to affective needs and varying cognitive styles of students) regarding their efficacy in raising student achievement. As you observe instruction in the classrooms of your school, compare what you see to what research says about the instructional methodologies that are effective in helping students to be numerate. Even the most definitive curriculum and well-written textbooks are merely ink and paper until a gifted teacher brings them to life. A firm grounding in mathematical knowledge along with instructional effectiveness are essential elements of raising student achievement, particularly the achievement of students with diverse needs.

> "Americans hold the notion that good teaching comes through artful and spontaneous interactions with students during lessons. This kind of on-the-fly decision making is made possible by the innate intuitions of 'natural' teachers. Such views minimize the importance of planning increasingly effective lessons and lend credence to the folk belief that good teachers are born, not made. If we really believe this, it is no wonder that teacher development is not a high priority."
> —Stigler & Hiebert, 1997, p. 16

Three mathematics educators set out to investigate what middle school students saw as the ideal mathematics teacher (Fleener, DuPree, & Craven, 1997). Using six *Far Side* cartoons by Gary Larson that humorously illustrated very different approaches to instruction, they asked 114 seventh- and eighth-graders to choose the cartoon that depicted the "ideal" mathematics teacher. The cartoons depicted teachers as a counselor/doctor, a game-show host, a taskmaster, a clown, a sage on the stage, and a facilitator.

More than half of the middle school students chose the ideal teacher to be a sage on the stage The researchers were surprised that students "lacked a lucid picture of the possibilities of mathematics classrooms being other than the teacher acting in the role of dispenser of knowledge. Many of the students, however, expressed comfort with this kind of teaching" (Fleener et al., 1997, p. 42). Even the students who *did* choose the "teacher as facilitator" cartoon as their ideal, described this teacher more as the dispenser of knowledge than as the guide, believing that the teacher's role was to

"teach the right solutions."

"teach [students] to work together to figure the solutions."

"answer questions and give advice."

"to explain what you are working on."

The researchers lamented that "despite exposure to innovative and open classroom activities and procedures by their own mathematics teacher, students' visions of the ideal mathematics classroom were limited by their prior mathematics learning experiences" (Fleener et al., 1997, p. 43).

In a similar study with preservice elementary education majors, the researchers found that the overwhelming majority of the students selected the cartoon labeled "teacher as facilitator," highlighting the active learning environment and investigative approach that were pictured as being keys to successful mathematics learning (Fleener & Reynolds, 1994). What might account for the marked differences between the students' and the preservice teachers' views regarding the preferred role for teachers in the mathematics classroom?

Perhaps these students have important empirical knowledge regarding some key instructional principles to which newly trained teachers ought to pay more attention:

▶ When students don't understand subject matter, they want coherent explanations, plenty of worked-out examples from which to draw conclusions, and problem-solving demonstrations, along with the strong sense that an adult is in charge.

▶ Students feel uneasy and stressful when a classroom is chaotic and their classmates (particularly a few disruptive ones) are in control rather than the teacher.

▶ Students (especially those with attention and learning disorders) grow agitated with noise and disturbances and fail to learn.

▶ Many students have a feeling of urgency about how much they have to learn and grow impatient with pooling their ignorance in groups where there is neither individual nor group accountability.

Perhaps these students have an intuitive sense of what Liping Ma (1999) describes in her brilliant volume on how little U.S. teachers really understand about mathematics: "The real mathematical thinking going on in a classroom, in fact, depends heavily on the teacher's understanding of mathematics" (p. 153).

Before you decide what to do *less* of and what to do *more* of in the classrooms of your school in order to raise mathematics achievement, evaluate the research in eight key areas:

> "A good vehicle....does not guarantee the right destination. The direction that students go with manipulatives depends largely on the steering of their teacher."
>
> —Ma, 1999, p. 5

1. The effectiveness of experiential hands-on learning

2. How best to structure discovery learning

3. The worth of calculators

4. The role of practice in mastering basic facts and algorithms

5. The effectiveness of direct instruction

6. The need for accountability in the use of cooperative learning

7. The need for effective instruction

8. The importance of teacher evaluation

## *Experiential Hands-On Learning: Does It Really Work?*

Before you commit exclusively to experiential hands-on learning with all of the attendant noise and movement of students doing, talking, and collaborating, read what these math educators and researchers have to say.

"It is now generally accepted that for mathematics teaching, surer foundations are laid when the child's thinking is closely linked with perceptual experiences acquired by doing things. 'I do and I understand' is a sound principle with which to begin, but one which needs care in application. Children can be quite happily and busily engaged in doing things without the activity leading very far. This may be the result of an ill-chosen apparatus, and there may be too many variables involved at once for sound judgments to be made. It may also be that the activity is not part of a progression of work on the topic. This is especially true, as far as mathematical work is concerned, of the activities at the sand tray or water trolley" (Thyer & Maggs, 1991, p. 1). "Using and applying mathematics must always be at the heart of learning the subject. But children need 'explanation' and teachers must organize their lessons and the pupils' activities in ways which give opportunities for them to provide careful, systematic, and appropriate explanation of mathematical concepts, procedures, and principles to groups of children. That many primary teachers neglect this aspect of teaching may possibly be associated with a prevailing primary ethos, which emphasises active learning and the needs of the individual pupil" (Haylock, 1995, p. 1).

Liping Ma (1999) interviewed Chinese and American teachers about how they would teach subtraction with regrouping. All but one of the 95 teachers interviewed mentioned manipulatives as one way they would teach this topic. Bundles of sticks, beans, and base 10 blocks were commonly mentioned. Of the American teachers, more than 80% focused their use of the manipulatives on the mechanics of computing the correct answer rather than on using them to help students gain the conceptual understanding of place value that is critical to being able to learn how to regroup. Unless teachers understand and are able to make meaningful connections between manipulatives and mathematical ideas, blocks, beans, and bundles are worthless. Only teachers who have a deep understanding of a mathematical topic can make the connection for students. American teachers seemed to believe that the mere presence of manipulatives in the classroom would create understanding. "In contrast with U.S. teachers, most Chinese teachers said that after students had used manipulatives they would have a class discussion, "a teaching strategy that requires more breadth and depth of a teacher's subject matter knowledge" (Ma, 1999, p. 27).

The *Review of High-Quality Experimental Mathematics Research* cited in Chapter 3 found four studies that investigated the effects of manipulatives upon mathematics achievement (Dixon, Carnine, Lee, Wallin, & Chard, 1998a, pp. 12–13). Three of those studies—all conducted in elementary schools—found no benefit to learning with manipulatives (Bright, Harvey, & Wheeler, 1981; Moody, Abell, & Bausell, 1971; Pasnak, Hansbarger, Dodson, Hart, & Blaha, 1996). One study, conducted with middle school students studying fractions and ratios, did find some positive benefits (Harrison, Brindley, and Bye, 1989). The jury is obviously still out on how the use of manipulatives contributes to mathematics achievement. Assuredly, one important consideration must be teachers' understanding of what the manipulatives are being used to teach. If teachers do not possess conceptual knowledge of the mathematics they are teaching, manipulatives will merely serve as distractors and playthings for students.

## Discovery Learning: How Best to Do It

Before you commit to children constructing their own meaning regarding mathematics through Discovery Learning (the inductive learning favored by constructivists and the 1989 NCTM standards), carefully consider these findings from *The Review of High Quality Experimental Mathematics Research* (Dixon et al., 1998a, pp. 17–18).

Three studies examined whether initial instruction should be given through a discovery mode, a guided discovery mode, or a direct (didactic) mode (Anastasiow, Sibley, Leonhardt, & Borich, 1970; Lackner, 1972; Olander & Robertson, 1973). A slight advantage appears to go to the guided discovery mode (see definition following) for some content and with higher-performing students, and to the direct mode for some content and with lower-performing students. There are no advantages indicated in these studies for a strict discovery mode (constructivist learning). Several additional studies in the review investigated some other aspect of mathematics instruction, but as part of their study found positive effects for explicit instruction as well (Dixon, Carnine, Lee, Wallin, & Chard, 1998b, p. 2).

*Guided discovery* may be a new term for you. It differs from pure discovery in that the teacher provides more prompts and assistance to the student along the way. The discussion, often a debate, regarding just how mathematics should be taught is often framed as it was in the earlier discussion about best practices: less whole class direct instruction versus more cooperative, collaborative activity or less passive student listening versus more active learning. The authors of the *Review of High Quality Experimental Mathematics Research* (Dixon et al., 1998a) describe a pattern that seems to maximize the strengths of both methodologies, providing an important blend or balance. The most effective mathematics lessons (i.e., lessons that resulted in increased student achievement) were characterized by a guided discovery instructional approach throughout all of the 110 studies surveyed.

The effective lesson was *not* the conventional-traditional lesson in which the students first sit passively and watch the teacher demonstrate a new algorithm or strategy, then work problems completely on their own. Neither were the effective lessons ones in which the teacher was merely the guide on the side, letting students discover and construct their own meaning. Discovery learning is often the most inefficient way to structure a lesson, though this loss of learning time would be more than justified if there were no other ways to reach the goal. "The increased effort and training time associated with discovery modes of instruction will not always be beneficial. Specifically, discovery learning per se does not seem to provide subjects with more insight into the information targeted for learning [i.e., a particular strategy]. Once learned, the information [i.e., a strategy] seems to be transferred with equal facility, regardless of whether or not it was discovered or explicated for the learner" (McDaniel & Schlager, 1990, p. 154).

Dixon and his colleagues (1998a) report that the lesson models for effective interventions most frequently followed a three-phase pattern. In the first phase, teachers not only demonstrated, but also explained, asked many questions, checked for understanding, or conducted discussions. In sharp contrast to the conventional model, students were almost always quite actively involved in the instruction during the initial phase. The second phase that was found in lessons that produced high achievement is an intermediate stage between learning something new and being proficient enough to apply that new knowledge independently. This is the *help phase* of the lesson, in which students gradually make a transition from teacher regulation to self-regulation. The specifics of this second phase vary considerably, from students helping one another collaboratively to high levels of teacher help with feedback and frequent *correctives* (additional explanation when students falter). In many cases, this second phase of instruction took up the majority of lesson time. Dixon and his colleagues (1998b) observed a third phase in effective lessons, one of individual accountability. "In contrast to the conventional model, in which the majority of lesson time was often taken up with students working independently on worksheets, independent work made up just a small percentage of lesson time in effective lessons. Often, the only independent activity was some form of an assessment activity. Frequently, individual accountability included an assessment of the students' ability to generalize or transfer their new knowledge to untaught applications. With very few exceptions, the studies did not simply assess students' ability to recall knowledge" (p. 8).

Good, Grouws, and Ebmeier (1983) suggest that it is both possible and essential for teachers to combine active learning and direct instruction—guided discovery—by doing the following:

- ▶ Constructing detailed long- and short-range plans
- ▶ Checking for mastery of prerequisite concepts and skills before introducing something new
- ▶ Making students aware of the major objectives of the lesson
- ▶ Spending at least half the period developing material in a way that actively engages all students and emphasizes understanding

▶ Involving students in important problem solving, estimation, mental math, and mathematical extensions related to the lesson

▶ Communicating the expectation that if students attend they will be able to master the material

▶ Providing clear, relevant examples as well as counter-examples

▶ Asking many "why," "how," and other high-level questions

▶ Being organized and maintaining a brisk pace to foster time on task

▶ Regularly assigning a small amount of homework to develop fluency with knowledge or skills previously mastered, to stimulate thinking about the next day's lesson, or to provide open-ended challenges

## The Use of Calculators: Boon or Boondoggle?

Before you decide to purchase calculators for every student in your school, examine the research, count the cost, and consider the practices of countries whose math performance far surpasses ours. Calculators do have their place in the classroom as a supplement to intense programs of computation instruction (Schnur & Lang, 1976; Standifer & Maples, 1981); however, we should take a page from the Japanese manual on wholesale calculator use starting in kindergarten. Calculators are not used before the fifth grade in Japan (Raimi & Braden, 1998). Calculators do not seem to be the "magic bullet" for higher achievement if we look at practices in high-achieving TIMSS countries.

> "If you haven't mastered basic arithmetic by hand, you can't do arithmetic at all—with or without calculators. Calculators are reliable, but people aren't; they hit wrong keys. You can't solve a problem unless you start with a general idea of the right answer. Otherwise you don't catch your errors, and you and your calculator are a menace."
> —Gelernter, 1998 [On-line]

> "Learning to calculate, especially with fractions and decimals, is more than 'getting the answer'; it is an exercise in reason and in the nature of our number system, and it underlies much that follows later in life. Only a person ignorant of all but the most trivial uses of calculation will believe that a calculator replaces—during the years of education—mental and verbal and written calculation."
> —Raimi & Braden, 1998

"Many of the higher-achieving countries both had less technology [calculators and computers] available and made less use of technology than did the United States. The case of the efficacy of using technology must remain at best 'not proven'" (Schmidt et al., 1999, p. 207).

## Practice: Nostalgia Math or Absolutely Essential?

Before you banish practice as nostalgia math, evaluate these findings. "The argument that practice to automatize the development of basic cognitive skills, such as fact retrieval, is unnecessary and unwanted in mathematics education fails to appreciate the importance of basic skills for mathematical development. As noted earlier, drill and practice provide an environment in which the child can notice regularities in mathematical operations and glean basic concepts from these regularities" (Briars & Siegler, 1984).

Teachers cannot simply dictate rote memorization of basic facts, however, and expect every child to master them. Overall, when regular classroom students in Grades 2 and 4 were taught strategies such as counting on, doubles, thinking more or less than a known fact, using 10, and recognition of the commutative property, they learned facts better and transferred and retained their knowledge better than did students in control groups that emphasized only drill and practice (Thornton, 1978). Eleven of the thirteen studies in *The Review of High Quality Experimental Research* found positive effects for particular types of strategy instruction, most particularly explicit instruction (Dixon et al., 1998a, p. 2).

> "One can no more use mathematical 'concepts' without a grounding in fact and experience, and indeed memorization and drill, than one can play a Beethoven sonata without exercise in scales and arpeggios."
> —Raimi & Braden, 1998

No educator believes in killing motivation through rote learning that denies the importance of understanding. Delete the word *drill* from your instructional lexicon and insert the word *practice* instead. "Nothing flies more in the face of the last 20 years of research than the assertion that practice is bad. All evidence, from the laboratory and from extensive case studies of professionals, indicates that real competence only comes with extensive practice [e.g., Ericsson, Krampe, & Tesche-Römer, 1993; Hayes, 1985]. In denying the critical role of practice one is denying children the very thing they need to achieve real competence. The instructional task is not to kill motivation by demanding drill, but to find tasks that provide practice while at the same time sustaining interest" (Anderson, Reder, & Simon, November, 1999 [On-line]).

"Many U.S. teachers . . . seem to believe that learning terms and practicing skills is not very exciting. We have watched them trying to jazz up the lesson and increase students' interest in nonmathematical ways: by being entertaining, by interrupting the lesson to talk about other things (last night's local rock concert, for example), or by setting the mathematics problems in a real-life or intriguing context— for example, measuring the circumference of a basketball. Teachers act as if student interest will be generated only by diversions outside of mathematics" (Stigler & Hiebert, 1999, p. 89).

Even when American teachers do expect their students to practice, they ask them to practice the wrong things. Although more than half of the Japanese, Korean, Czech, and Hungarian eighth-grade mathematics teachers surveyed for the TIMSS study reported having students practice writing equations in every lesson or most lessons, only a third of U.S. teachers reported practice in writing equations. American teachers reported that their eighth-grade students were still practicing computation, which should have been practiced and mastered earlier (Schmidt et al., 1999, p. 73).

## Sage on the Stage or Guide on the Side?

Before you completely eradicate whole-class, teacher-directed instruction, consider its effectiveness in raising student achievement, especially for at-risk students. Direct instruction is often misconstrued by those who do not thoroughly understand its approach to instructional design as rote learning without meaning. The theory upon which direct instruction is based is fully cognizant that students are not empty vessels that teachers can fill at will. Clearly, if a learner is not able to make sense out of what the teacher says and does, learning will not occur. There is a major difference, however, between the way the radical constructivists believe students construct meaning and the way in which those who practice direct instruction see it occurring—the major role the teacher plays. "The way in which teachers organize the learning environment determines how successful learners will be in constructing the meaning that teachers intend to convey" (Stein et al., 1997, p. 2).

One of the most frequently voiced objections to direct instruction is its use of carefully scripted lessons. "[The] preparing and rehearsing of formats prior to their use with students allows the teacher, during instruction, to focus full attention on students. Rather than being distracted by thinking of additional examples or the next steps to present, the teacher can concentrate on monitoring the students' responses, correcting mistakes, and keeping motivation high" (Stein et al., 1997, p. 6).

The research on the effectiveness of a direct instruction approach to teaching mathematics is impressive (Abt Associates, 1976). Nine early childhood approaches to educating primary children were evaluated as a part of Project Follow-Through: child-centered, responsive education (Far West Lab); language experiences (Tucson Early Education); child development (Bank Street); direct instruction (University of Oregon); behavior modification (University of Kansas); Piagetian (cognitive curriculum—High Scope Foundation); parent education (University of Florida); open education (Educational Development Corporation); and bilingual (Southwest Education). Third-graders who had participated in a particular approach since kindergarten were evaluated using the Metropolitan Achievement Test's math subtests. Scores in mathematics for students who experienced direct instruction from kindergarten through third grade were three-fourths to a full standard deviation ahead of the scores for students from most of the other approaches. The 20th percentile was used as a common baseline because it is the average expectation for children from economically disadvantaged backgrounds. Even more significant is the fact that the direct instruction students performed almost at the national norm, an accomplishment that demonstrates the potential for all students to be successful in mathematics (Silbert, Carnine, & Stein, 1981, p. 483).

## Cooperative Learning:
## Accountability Is the Key to Success

Before you mandate cooperative learning as a schoolwide strategy for learning mathematics, make sure that you and your teachers fully understand the critical differences between cooperative learning as it is being practiced in many American classrooms and the system as it is used in Japan. Make sure your teachers are committed and are trained to include the added instruction and monitoring that must take place from the first day of school to enable students to function as effective group members.

In Japan, "teachers make an explicit effort during the early months of elementary school to teach children techniques and skills that will allow them to function effectively in a group. Children learn how to move from one activity to another, how to arrange the contents of their desks so that they can find things easily, how to pay attention, how to follow directions, and how to speak loudly and clearly so that they can be understood" (Stevenson & Stigler, 1992, p. 62),

TIMSS researchers describe a typical mathematics lesson in Japan: Small groups of students, *hans,* were commonly formed for discussion and activity purposes during lessons, then often worked further on problems, after which each han was asked to present its results to the whole class. A han is a fairly stable student group, changing only once or twice during the year. The Japanese hans differ substantially from the way cooperative groups are structured in the United States, in which there is often little group or individual accountability. Cooperative learning groups are frequently misused in American classrooms, particularly by teachers who have been instructed to use groups but have never been given the kind of extensive training that is needed to structure and facilitate such groups for improved achievement. In Japan, children have regular experiences working together with the members of their group. They learn about being responsible to and for each other. Stevenson and Stigler (1992) suggest that "since this use of groups is a consistent part of the characteristic pedagogical approaches used by most Japanese mathematics and science teachers in most grades, the experience of how to work responsibly and effectively in groups is cumulative and helps account for the comparative efficiency of the Japanese group work" (p. 96).

Eleven experimental studies related to group work were identified in the *Review of High Quality Experimental Mathematics Research* (Dixon et al., 1998a). The findings are quite positive for some forms of cooperative peer study. Cooperative teamwork can be used effectively as a motivational technique in which the reinforcement and evaluation systems are based on the team's performance. In addition to the effects of cooperative group work on motivation, the other powerful dimension of cooperative group work relates to instructional interactions. "Highly structured, interactive group work seems clearly to mediate the transition from initial teacher-directed instruction to self-regulation. In general, students support one another in group work. More specifically, that support takes the form of more (and, sometimes, different) explanations, more opportunities to respond, additional opportunities for feedback, and the potential (realized in these studies) for better focus upon the tasks at hand" (Dixon et al., 1998a, pp. 14–16).

Coordinate and articulate your approach to cooperative learning in every classroom; make it part of a larger, well-structured instructional system.


## Effective Teaching:
## The Key to Raising Math Achievement

Before you schedule your next round of teacher observations, review the teacher effectiveness literature. Then read about the instructional methodologies used by mathematics teachers in other countries (Ma, 1999; Stigler & Hiebert, 1999). Think about ways in which you can help your teachers polish and perfect their teaching methodologies.

The following categories summarize the critical aspects of effective instruction.


1. Instruction is guided by a preplanned curriculum (Venezky & Winfield, 1979). This characteristic speaks to the need for objectives, time lines, and planning in determining what will be done daily in the classroom. If teachers don't know where they're going, neither they nor their students will get there.


2. There are high expectations for student learning (Phi Delta Kappa, 1980). Students are not expected to fail because of their SES, their parents' educational level, or the neighborhood where they live. All students are expected to learn.


3. Students are carefully oriented to lessons (Stallings, 1979). Students in today's classrooms are frequently at a loss as to what is going on during class. Students must be told in advance what is expected of them and be prepared for learning.

4. Instruction is clear and focused (Lortie, 1975). This seems like such an obvious statement, but my years of classroom observation have led me to believe otherwise. When I, an experienced former teacher and a principal, had no clue about what was being taught, how could students be expected to figure it out?

5. Learning progress is monitored closely (Evertson, 1982). Teachers hold students accountable and use frequent assessments to see if what they're doing is working. They use this information to modify their instruction.

6. When students don't understand, they are retaught (Rosenshine, 1983). When everyone fails a test, effective teachers figure out what went wrong with their teaching, then reteach using an alternative approach.

7. Class time is used for learning (Stallings, 1980). Reduce the assemblies, field trips, fund-raisers, and intercom announcements and teach. Determine how much of each math teacher's class time is used to do homework. Teachers in the United States typically assign homework (meant to be done at home as suggested by its name), then give students large chunks of class time for doing the assignment. It is the dominant lesson component in U.S. classrooms, whereas in Japan, class time is predominantly used for new instruction (Schmidt et al., 1999, pp. 67–68). One must ask whether U.S. teachers believe students are incapable of working independently, whether they are reluctant to ask too much of students, whether they have planned nothing better to do with the time, or whether they simply feel no sense of urgency to accomplish as much as they can in the short time they have to work directly with students.

8. There are smooth, efficient classroom routines (Brophy, 1979). Efficient classrooms seem to run by themselves with seamless transitions and little "administrivia."

9. The instructional groups formed in the classroom fit instructional needs (Stallings, 1979). Ability-based groups formed in kindergarten should not remain unchanged through high school. Nor should students who need more specialized instruction always be expected to learn from brighter students in cooperative groups.

10. Standards for classroom behavior are explicit (Anderson, 1980). Rules, expectations, and consequences are made clear to students from day one.

11. Personal interactions between teachers and students are positive (Rutter, Maughan, Mortimore, & Ouston, 1979). Effective teachers really care about their students and demonstrate this care in thousands of brief interactions daily.

12. Incentives and rewards for students are used to promote excellence (Emmer & Evertson, 1981). This practice has come under a lot of fire from educators who are opposed to competition because everybody isn't a winner (Kohn, 1986). In my opinion and experience, if students work and achieve, they will be winners. When excellence is defined by objective standards and not by peer comparison and the rewards are appropriate for the level of the student, incentives and rewards work (Northwest Regional Education Laboratory, 1984, pp. 3–6).

There are a variety of ways in which you can help your teachers improve their teaching methodologies in mathematics. Schedule a class on the teaching of mathematics to be held on your campus. Invite high school teachers or university professors to provide content-area instruction in mathematics where appropriate. Invite a teacher who consistently motivates all students to be successful in mathematics to teach a model lesson. For those teachers who are frustrated with their lack of mathematical knowledge or are math-phobic, establish a small library of resource materials. Encourage, even insist, that teachers observe in the classrooms of master teachers.

Plan staff development that focuses on overall teaching effectiveness. These sessions can be facilitated by master teachers or organized around a self-study cooperative learning group. When you see teachers whose instruction is unfocused, confused, and poorly planned, provide help through mentors or coaches, visits to effective classrooms, demonstration teaching, and targeted staff development. "U.S. teachers rarely have the opportunity to observe other teachers in action and are rarely observed by other teachers. For whatever reason, teaching in the United States is considered a private, not a public, activity. The consequences of this isolation are severe" (Stigler & Hiebert, 1999, p. 123). Teachers can describe how they teach "problem solving," but only when colleagues actually observe each other's lessons do teachers really know if they have a common definition and approach to instruction in problem solving. Make yourself available as an instructional resource by spending time in classrooms, both observing and teaching. Form discussion groups around the topic of mathematics instruction. Pull out all the stops to let your teachers know that you support them but that you expect them to provide high-quality instruction. Effective teaching is the key to raising mathematics achievement.

Allocate time (even if you have to hire substitutes to release teachers from their classes) for teachers to regularly talk with one other about math instruction. Use resources creatively to buy time for teachers to plan lessons jointly and then observe each other teaching them. Teachers in the United States have far less structured support to help them improve their teaching of mathematics than do their counterparts in other countries (Black & Atkins, 1996). Teachers in the United States often work in isolation and seldom have the opportunity to receive feedback on their teaching performance that is formative rather than summative in nature. Peer observation and discussion of lesson design is one way to improve mathematics instruction, but it is rarely used. Arrange for a joint planning session for all of the teachers of a grade level or subject. Choose a topic (e.g., double-digit multiplication or the addition of fractions) and ask each teacher to plan a lesson on the topic that can be discussed and critiqued by the group. Follow up with opportunities for classroom observation and further discussion so that the lesson can be fine-tuned. This kind of teacher interaction happens regularly in Japan where specific lessons, particularly on topics that students find challenging, are polished and perfected.

## What to Do About Ineffective Teachers

If you are tempted to ignore ineffective teachers, pause to think about the effects on a student, particularly an at-risk student, of spending a year with an ineffective teacher. A statistical model developed by William Sanders and his colleagues at the University of Tennessee, the Tennessee Value-Added Assessment System (TVAAS), has yielded some startling findings that confirm what parents have always believed

(Sanders & Rivers, 1996): When children get a bad teacher for one year, it hurts; when children get a bad teacher two years in a row, their educational progress can be in jeopardy. In Sanders and Rivers' study, fifth-graders who had three years of teachers who were judged ineffective by their supervisors averaged 54 to 60 percentile points lower in achievement than did students who had teachers judged effective. And the results of the teacher effects (bad or good) carried forward and accumulated for as long as two years. When you uncover problems in the course of your observations, don't look the other way. If your teachers are uncomfortable with teaching mathematics because they are math-phobic or have been poorly trained, schedule an intensive staff development program that is focused on mathematics content.

> "Americans, it turned out, were more willing than were Japanese and Chinese to attribute children's academic successes and failures to innate abilities and disabilities; the Asians referred more to environmental facts and children's own effort in their explanations of school performance."
> —Stevenson & Stigler, 1992, p. 8
>
> ————◇————
>
> "It seems to me probable that the proportion of grammar school children incapable of pursuing geometry, algebra, and a foreign language would turn out to be much smaller than we now imagine."
> —Eliot, 1892/1961, pp. 52–53

There are occasions, however, when, despite all you do, a teacher remains ineffective. Escalating parental complaints, a continuing pattern of low student gain scores from year to year, and a growing collection of unsatisfactory evaluation ratings tell the story. That's when it's time to *literally* change the teacher: reassign that individual to give them a new perspective; counsel with them regarding their career goals; or work with legal counsel to recommend dismissal.

Thus far, we have considered four important alterable variables: curriculum, connection of curriculum, textbooks, and teaching methodologies. There are two remaining variables to examine before we can sum up the equation: our expectations for how much of the content students can learn and do and how we assess what students have mastered.

## Change Your Expectations

Changing your own and your teachers' expectations for how much of the content every student can learn will send achievement skyrocketing. I guarantee it. Changing educators' expectations is difficult because it means facing the reality that heretofore their expectations have been low. That can be a distressing experience for some folks, especially if they find it difficult to let go of long-standing beliefs and values. Changing students' expectations is even more difficult. Students who have been led to believe that they can't, won't.

The most dramatic example of the effects of high expectations on student achievement can be seen in "the best teacher in America," Jaime Escalante (Mathews, 1988). The movie *Stand and Deliver* brought Escalante's story to life on the big screen. The 44-year-old Bolivian began his teaching career in the United States at Garfield High School in East Los Angeles, a school where the inalterable variables were crushing. When Escalante started teaching at Garfield, 80% of the students qualified for free and reduced lunch, and the student body was primarily Latino. At least 25% of the students came from families that received Aid to Families with Dependent Children. Escalante didn't pay any attention to the demographics. He wanted to teach calculus to his students. What's more, he wanted them to take the AP (Advanced Placement) calculus test and get passing grades. Against all odds, he succeeded. Jay Mathews, the Los Angeles bureau chief of the *Washington Post,* tells Escalante's story in a compelling biography. "The story of Jaime Escalante and Garfield High School says to teachers, principals, parents, and students that those handicaps [the demographics of which we spoke] can be overcome. They can achieve results they never dreamed of. All they need is the drive and impatience and love that pushes a school and its students far beyond their assumed limits" (Mathews, 1988, p. 5).

If your teachers doubt that achievement can be raised in your school, rent *Stand and Deliver* at your local video store and show it at your next faculty meeting. Buy Matthews's book and make it required reading for every teacher. What Escalante was able to do was all about expectations. With low expectations, at-risk students simply fail and drop out. We can do better than we have done with almost every student, but especially with our most at-risk students. Buy multiple copies of the 36-page booklet *No Excuses: Seven Principals of Low-Income Schools Who Set the Standard for High Achievement* (Carter, 1999). It provides concrete examples of schools around the country that are succeeding in spite of the odds.

If your teachers still think that achievement can't be raised because your students just aren't smart enough, point them to the Institute for Learning at the University of Pittsburgh, where researchers have been working with schools around the country to help teachers get students on an upward, "getting smarter" spiral. "It is possible to help students develop learning-oriented goals and an incremental view of intelligence and thus set them on the upward spiral by which they can become smarter and deliver the kinds of high-level academic achievement everyone is hoping for. To do this, we need to create effort-based schools in which academic rigor and a thinking curriculum permeate the school day for every student" (Resnick, 1999, p. 39).

We have far too many dropouts. Oh, the students I'm talking about don't actually drop out of school; they drop out of mathematics. These students decide very early in their schooling careers that they just don't get it. Maybe they missed some critical learning in an early grade (e.g., place value). Maybe they never mastered the basic facts and algorithms that enable fluent and automatic problem solving. Often, a student's mathematics difficulties are actually reading and writing deficiencies. And sometimes math has just acquired a bad reputation and is mistakenly thought to be a subject only for nerds, geeks, and brains.

Between 20% and 25% of students who complete high school are actually mathematics dropouts (Dossey, Lindquist, & Chamber, 1988). Kasten & Howe (1988) describe this not insubstantial group of young people as "nominal mathematics students." They stay in high school and may even attend college, but their mathematics preparation does not adequately allow them maximum educational and occupational choices. Math dropouts disappear into the cracks of high school and, unlike those students who actually withdraw from school, cause scarcely a ripple. They are rarely reported in any official documents. Math teachers certainly aren't worried about them. Who wants to teach disinterested, unmotivated, and ill-prepared students? Administrators aren't concerned either. If all of these kids suddenly registered for AP calculus, there would be a severe staffing problem. About the only folks who actually seem to care are the researchers who track national assessment scores over time. They have hypothesized that the mathematics dropouts are one of the major reasons why mathematics achievement in the United States is so low (Kasten & Howe, 1988).

Our expectations as educators aren't nearly high enough. We let our students get by with learning far less than their international counterparts. That's not their fault, it's ours. When TIMSS researchers examined the scores U.S. students received at the end of third and seventh grades and at the end of fourth and eighth grades, the data revealed very little academic growth. Students might as well have been sitting in a study hall as in a math class. That's depressing. Where's the academic press (the constant articulation of high expectations accompanied by teaching that helps students be successful)? "Less than 40 percent of U.S. teachers provided 20 minutes or more instruction in *new* [italics added] material during a class period. Japanese teachers, by contrast, spent most of their time on a combination of instruction on new material and on seatwork, which was for the most part, actively tied to the instruction of new material during the course of a lesson" (Schmidt et al., 1999, p. 71). As instructional leaders we must investigate if this is the case in our schools, then do something about it by improving achievement from the earliest grades and systematically eliminating low-level mathematics classes.

Establishing high expectations is something everybody talks about, but how does one actually do it? Alan Jones, principal of West Chicago High School put it this way: "To foster academic achievement, schools need to do more than simply set demanding standards for children. They need to structure academic experiences in a way that enhances students' sense of efficacy. Good instruction helps students of all levels, regardless of teacher expectations" (personal communication, February 15, 1996).

If you are trying to raise achievement, everything that is done must focus on students' learning. "Improving complex systems, such as teaching, requires a relentless focus on the bottom-line goals—in this case, students' learning—and a commitment to evaluate changes with respect to these goals" (Stigler & Hiebert, 1999, p. 133). What can administrators do to communicate high expectations to students and create an environment in which they have every opportunity to learn? McEwan (1998b) offers the following:

▶ Establish inclusive classrooms that send the message that all students can learn.

▶ Provide extended learning opportunities for students who need them (e.g., Saturday school, after-school tutorials, summer school, peer tutors, computer-assisted instruction, and motivational programs such as Accelerated Math).

▶ Observe and reinforce positive teacher behaviors in the classroom that ensure an academically demanding climate and an orderly, well-managed classroom.

▶ Send messages to students in a variety of ways and at every opportunity that they can succeed.

▶ Establish policies on student progress relative to homework, grading, monitoring of progress, remediation, reporting progress, and retention/promotion.

▶ Make sure these policies are communicated to parents and uniformly and fairly implemented by teachers.

▶ Ensure that time is being used effectively (e.g., minimize interruptions and reinforce teachers who use time wisely).

▶ Assign the very best teachers to the students who are most at risk.

▶ Establish motivational programs, like a Mathematics Career Day, or competitive programs that make learning meaningful, like Math Counts (see Chapter 7 for further ideas).

▶ Create a safe and secure environment in which there are no distractions for either students or teachers (pp. 44–56).

The final alterable variable to consider in raising mathematics achievement concerns how we assess student mastery of content. What gets measured gets done!

*Change How You Assess*

There are two ways to assess student mastery of content—during the process of learning (formative) and after the learning is supposed to have taken place (summative). Both types of testing are important. Obviously, if a teacher wants to make on-the-spot changes in instructional methodologies or determine if reteaching is necessary, formative testing is essential. Summative testing can tell you *that* something is wrong, but only formative, curriculum-based assessment can tell you precisely *what* is wrong. Consider the elementary teacher in Tennessee whose students made unsatisfactory gains in mathematics on the state assessment. She had the same reaction that most of us have when our students don't do well; she looked for reasons other than her own teaching. But once this bright and dedicated teacher got over her initial distress, she began to think about what she could do differently. She knew she was a good teacher; she just needed to find out why her students' scores didn't reflect it. She looked at the problem from a variety of angles and decided to do more formative assessments. Bingo! She discovered that many students would learn the day's or the week's lesson and then promptly forget it. She began to test and track her students several weeks after a lesson was taught. Those that had forgotten critical skills were retaught. In subsequent years, using a more rigorous formative assessment system, her students' gains scores have nearly tripled from that first disappointing year (Coffey, 1999, p. 6A).

When all the parts of this equation are added together—coordinated and articulated content, well-written textbooks and instructional materials that are aligned with the content, research-based instructional methodologies used by effective teachers, and high expectations for students—the answer ought to equal meaningful high achievement. Well, the equation *will* add up to meaningful high achievement if what is being taught and the summative test that is being used to measure what students know and can do are actually aligned. As many a state has discovered, it's not that easy to get 2 + 2 to add up to 4. If what is being taught is challenging but students are being tested with a test that is too easy, high test scores are no cause for rejoicing.

The state of California hired William Schmidt of TIMSS fame to see how closely the Stanford Achievement Test mathematics subtest (the test being used to assess mathematics achievement) aligned with the state's math standards. The study found that the standardized test contained too much basic arithmetic, especially at the eighth-grade level. The state standards emphasized higher-level concepts (Boser, 1999, p. 10).

In Texas, evaluators found that the Texas Assessment of Academic Skills (TAAS) mathematics exams and the end-of-course algebra 1 exams contained many low-level items and the rising achievement of students on the test was not as spectacular as first believed. "In summary," the evaluators noted, "the system of mathematics achievement assessment in Texas emerges as a powerful model but one that is too highly focused on minimal achievement. The incentives for improvement that accompany the state assessment system do not emphasize high achievement sufficiently" (Clopton, Bishop, & Klein, 1998 [On-line]).

Achievement may be very low for a variety of reasons—teaching objectives do not match what is being tested, instruction is substandard, or students are failing to take the outcome of the test seriously. In the first administration of the AIMS (Arizona Instrument to Measure Standards) high school graduation test in Arizona, 9 of every 10 students failed the mathematics portion of the test (Corella & Tapia, 1999, p. 1A). Some speculated that because the test does not impact high school graduation status until 2002, both students and teachers feel they have time to remedy the abysmal showing. Others were dismayed that even in some of the state's premier high schools more than three quarters of the students failed the math test.

Educators must be vigilant regarding the quality of state assessments. Work with officials in your state department of education or lobby elected officials in the legislature to explain the folly of wasting taxpayers' money, along with teachers' and students' valuable instructional time, by requiring tests that are too easy, too difficult, too cumbersome, or too subjective or tests that do not address the critical academic learnings of a discipline. Communicate to officials the importance of maintaining an unbroken history of longitudinal data in documenting improvement efforts. Convince them to do the job right the first time so that the state's (and your school's) data history remains coherent. Too many states have used teachers and administrators as pawns in their fumbling attempts to get it right. Teachers and students grow cynical when state assessments continually come and go, changing every time a new administration or state superintendent is elected. If your efforts to raise achievement are not fully supported by well-constructed, rigorous assessments that measure the critical mathematical knowledge and skills students must have, communicate your concerns to the decision makers in your state capital. If possible, obtain copies or samples of actual tests and evaluate them so that your objections can be as informed as possible.

## What Do the Experts Recommend Be Changed?

Those who have studied schools in the countries where mathematics achievement far surpasses that of the United States have considered the question of what might be changed to increase mathematics achievement in the United States. There are four important books to consult for this global perspective: *The Learning Gap: Why Our Schools Are Failing and What We Can Learn from Japanese and Chinese Education* (Stevenson & Stigler, 1992); *The Teaching Gap: Best Ideas from the World's Teachers for Improving Education in the Classroom* (Stigler & Hiebert, 1999); *Knowing and Teaching Elementary Mathematics: Teachers' Understanding of Fundamental Mathematics in China and the United States* (Ma, 1999); and *Facing Consequences: Using TIMSS for a Closer Look at U.S. Mathematics and Science Education* (Schmidt et al., 1999).

Stevenson and Stigler (1992) make the following suggestions in *The Learning Gap: Why Our Schools Are Failing and What We Can Learn from Japanese and Chinese Education:*

1. Free teachers. "Until teachers have adequate time to prepare lessons, work outside of class with individual students and perfect their teaching practices by interacting with each other and with master teachers, it is going to be difficult, if not impossible to change what children learn and do in school" (p. 207).

2. Improve teacher training. "The more teachers know about what they are teaching, the more they can contribute to their students" (p. 209).

3. Make systematic use of learning principles. "There is evidence that children learn most effectively when "they have a teacher who, among other behaviors, leads them to make discoveries; they are presented with lessons that are well scripted and well organized; they are presented with multiple examples of a concept so that they can deduce the underlying principle; and they are provided with opportunities to practice what they have been taught" (pp. 209–210).

4. Teach to the group. "Rather than teaching different lessons to different groups of children and thereby limiting the time any one group spends with the teacher, teachers should try to spend as much time as possible working with the whole class" (p. 211).

5. Consider increasing class size. "We believe that many improvements in elementary education could be accomplished if the average class size were slightly increased and the savings used to expand teachers' opportunities for perfecting their teaching and for interacting with other teachers" (p. 212).

6. Revise textbooks. "Curricula need not return year after year to the same material" (p. 213). The so-called spiral curriculum that some textbook series advertise could more accurately be labeled a *curricular curriculum*. Textbooks should *progress* in accordance with a set of standards rather than circle back to the same concepts over and over.

*The Teaching Gap: Best Ideas from the World's Teachers for Improving Education in the Classroom* (Stigler & Hiebert, 1999) uses the TIMSS video project to highlight the best ideas from the world's teachers for improving education in the classrooms of the United States. The authors suggest three important ways in which U.S. schools might improve the teaching of mathematics:

1. Maintain a constant focus on student learning. "Reforms in the United States often are tied to particular theories of teaching or to educational fads instead of to specific learning outcomes. Because of this, success often is measured by the degree to which teachers implement recommended practices. Someone is marked as a good teacher because he or she uses cooperative groups or concrete manipulatives, instead of on the basis of his or her students' successful learning" (p. 121).

2. Focus on the direct improvement of teaching in context. "As useful as educational research might be, it is notoriously difficult to bridge the gap separating researchers and practitioners. Japanese teachers function both as teachers and researchers, making it unnecessary to translate one into the other" (p. 122).

3. Make the improvement of teaching a collaborative effort. "By working in groups to improve instruction, teachers are able to develop a shared language for describing and analyzing classroom teaching and to teach each other about teaching" (p. 123).

In a third and very thought-provoking book about the teaching of mathematics, Liping Ma (1999) makes several critical recommendations regarding how we can help our teachers to increase their mathematical knowledge (pp. 146–153).

1. "Address teacher knowledge and student learning at the same time." Teachers must be learning and studying the content of elementary mathematics even as they are teaching it. This is the only way that mathematics learning for students can improve.

2. "Enhance the interaction between teachers' study of school mathematics and how to teach it." Ma's study found that while Chinese teachers develop a deep understanding of mathematics at the same time they are teaching it, experienced U.S. teachers knew no more about math content than brand-new teachers. Ma suggests two reasons that U.S. teachers do not develop a deeper understanding as they teach. First, the teachers believe that elementary math is basically pretty easy and superficial. Second, they feel that once they have obtained a degree they don't need to learn anymore about mathematics. U.S. teachers are not oriented toward approaching their preparation for the teaching of and their teaching of mathematics as learners. They often teach a lesson the same way in their 20th year of teaching as in their first year.

3. "Refocus teacher preparation." Ma points out that a vicious circle exists in which low-quality mathematics education, low-quality teacher knowledge of mathematics, and low-quality teacher preparation continuously reinforce and undermine poor mathematics achievement.

4. "Understand the role that curricular materials, including textbooks, might play in reform." Although teachers need the freedom to move beyond textbooks, the notion that teachers should design their own lessons, toss out textbooks, and have an "antagonistic relationship with textbooks" is counter-productive, especially when connections and alignment between grade levels is paramount.

5. "Understand the key to reform: Whatever the form of classroom interactions might be, they must focus on substantive mathematics." If you want to improve mathematics achievement, the focus must be on the mathematics—on achievement, not activity.

This is one of the most exciting times to be talking about and implementing mathematics improvement. The best minds in the world are evaluating the data, reflecting on the issues, and suggesting possibilities for further investigation. In *Facing Consequences: Using TIMSS for a Closer Look at U.S. Mathematics and Science Education,* William Schmidt and his colleagues (1999) advance six critical "stories" that emerged from their detailed study of mathematics teaching and achievement in the United States.

1. *Curriculum matters.* What we teach is what we get. The evidence is clear that when you teach a myriad of topics and treat none of them in depth, achievement suffers.

2. *Some get it and some don't.* Students across the United States have significantly different opportunities to take advanced mathematics courses and/or to do well in mathematics. The students who have the good fortune to live in the suburban Chicago districts that comprise the First in the World Consortium, for example, are far more likely to graduate from high school with four years of mathematics under their belt than their inner city counterparts 40 miles to the south. "Some children achieve less, not because they work less hard or have less ability to master mathematics, but

because of where they attend schools and the policies that determine which educational possibilities they will have access to" (p. 216).

3. *It's not just how long you make it, but how you make it long.* The TIMSS researchers chose this slogan from a cigarette commercial to capture the idea that increasing the time you teach mathematics is pointless unless you substantially change the way you teach it. Time in and of itself is not the problem with U.S. mathematics instruction. We spend about the same amount of time teaching math as other countries in the world. We just teach it in substantially different ways.

4. *Pedagogy is conditional.* Having said that we must change the way we teach, we cannot just rush out to reproduce what we have observed in other countries without considering the cultural context. "The use and effectiveness of pedagogical approaches are situated inextricably in culture contexts in complex ways and these cannot be treated as unconditioned strategies equally at home in different cultural contexts" (pp. 199, 217).

5. *Mobility matters.* Kids move around a lot. "A significant proportion of students really do end the year in different classrooms than those in which they began it" (p. 217). The more we can standardize math curriculum and instruction, the more likely we are to raise achievement.

6. *Connections count.* This is one of the most challenging ideas that the TIMSS researchers leave us with. On the one hand, they suggest that American students seem to need a considerable amount of stimulus to hold their interest during a typical math lesson, and on the other hand, they posit the idea that too many bells and whistles in the classroom soon leave students feeling that the content is superficial and unimportant. The challenge for teachers is to connect curriculum to students' lives in sincere and meaningful ways without minimalizing the commitment and effort that is needed to achieve in mathematics.

You have no doubt been compiling a to-do list while reading Chapter 4 or, at the very least, making some mental notes about what might need to change in your school to raise mathematics achievement. Before you form a task force to develop your Mathematics Improvement Plan (more about that in Chapter 6), focus on the essential learnings of mathematics from kindergarten through 12th grade. Chapter 5 will help you evaluate the content of your current mathematics program against a program that has the potential to produce higher achievement.

# The Essentials of
# Math Achievement

*"Math is right up there with snakes, public speaking, and heights."*

—Burns, 1998, p. ix

*"Only in the United States do people believe that learning mathematics depends on special ability. In other countries, students, parents, and teachers all expect that most students can master mathematics if only they work hard enough. The record of accomplishment in these countries—and in some intervention programs in the United States—shows that most students can learn much more mathematics than is commonly assumed in this country."*

—National Research Council, 1989, p. 10

*"The important thing to remember about mathematics is not to be frightened. It isn't as difficult as the mathematical priesthood sometimes pretends. Whenever I feel intimidated, I always remember Silvanus Thompson's dictum in Calculus Made Easy: 'What one fool can do, another can.'*

—Dawkins, 1986, p. 67

Many individuals and organizations are telling you what mathematics content to teach in your school and how to go about teaching it: the mathematics educators who teach beginning teachers how to teach mathematics; the teachers who teach in your school; the cognitive scientists and researchers who study how we think and learn; the policy makers in Washington, D.C.; organizations like the National Science

Foundation and the NCTM; your own state department of education; and the textbook publishers. If you're not confused, you may be out of touch with reality.

When I set out to write this book, I fantasized about opening a brand-new school, one in which I could erase all of the mistakes I had made in the past and take advantage of the very latest in research regarding mathematics. The curriculum and teaching methodologies used in my dream school would be the very best I could find, and the teachers would be handpicked for their love of mathematics. They would share a deep desire for students to appreciate and think about mathematics in new ways as well as to see the relationships between mathematical ideas. The school would enroll a broad cross-section of students from a variety of backgrounds and home environments. The buses would roll in each morning bringing students from every corner of the city.

In the course of my quest for the very best, I have consulted a variety of mathematics educators, talked with professors of mathematics, corresponded with individuals who use mathematics in their professional careers, interacted with classroom teachers who successfully motivate students to achieve in math, viewed the TIMSS video to see examples of mathematics instruction in various countries, surveyed most states' standards documents for mathematics and reviewed evaluations of the remaining few, examined textbooks in every category, read the NCTM Standards—old and new—and perused reams of TIMSS reports, books, and summaries. Here's what I want my ideal K–12 school to be and do based on my investigation.

*The School Essentials: Ways of Being*

There are three behaviors, or ways of being, that are essential to raising mathematics achievement: a focus on student achievement, a total commitment to meaningful curriculum, and a concentration on collaboration.

## Maintain a Complete Focus on Student Achievement

If your goal is to have high student achievement regardless of the variables that often presage low achievement, keep your faculty and students constantly focused on the established learning outcomes. A basketball commentator recently described the frenetic attempts of a team to score as they raced up and down the court. They were turning the ball over and constantly missing shots; they were working very hard but getting nowhere. "What this team needs," the announcer opined, "is less activity and more achievement." That phrase should be the mantra of every school that desires to raise achievement—less activity and more achievement. Fewer programs, fewer reform initiatives, and fewer cutting-edge innovations. A total and constant focus on learning must replace "doing things" and "being busy." Every teacher must regard each day as a singular opportunity for students to gain additional understanding; the teacher must carefully plan every lesson to maximize learning. Teaching and learning must be at the top of everyone's agenda; nothing must interrupt the process. Less activity and more achievement.

In their book, *The Teaching Gap,* Stigler & Hiebert (1999) relate an experience they had while watching a videotape of a U.S. mathematics lesson with a Japanese member of the research team. An American teacher was standing at the chalkboard demonstrating a procedure when a voice boomed over the intercom regarding an impending change of bus schedules. The Japanese team member was stunned and turned to ask why that voice was interrupting the teacher. The Americans replied, "Oh, that's nothing, just a P.A. announcement." The Japanese teacher was incredulous. He explained that no one would ever think of bursting into a classroom over the intercom in Japan. It would ruin the flow of the lesson (p. 55). To create a focus on student achievement, hold the act of teaching sacred.

The *only* real way to know if you're producing achievement as opposed to activity is to measure through regular curriculum-based assessments what students know and can do. Assess frequently enough so that the results can inform instruction, then be ready to change the game plan if necessary to achieve the goal. I believe it was another basketball coach who said, "If you keep on doing what you've always done, you'll keep on getting what you always got." Therefore, if students are not making the desired progress or learning what they are supposed to learn, something has to change (instructional methodologies, grouping, amount of time devoted to instruction, teacher-student ratio, textbooks, the quality of student practice, etc.).

## Develop a Total Commitment to Meaningful Curriculum

All standards are not created equal. All standards do not give teachers "marching orders" they can actually follow. A standard must be clear, definite, and testable. If it is not, how can a teacher commit to teaching it to students with the goal of mastery? How can a brand-new teacher even begin to know what to do? If a standard is fuzzy, indefinite, or incapable of being evaluated, most teachers will ignore it or substitute one of their own choosing in its place. What they choose may be better or worse. It may or may not be connected and articulated with any other teacher's chosen standards. A verbose or repetitive curriculum document invites teachers to tuck it away on a shelf to gather dust, rather than consulting it daily as a road map for where to head next. I would choose the 47-page Japanese Standards Document for kindergarten through 12th grade (Japan Society of Mathematical Education, 1990) or the 63-page California Standards Document (California State Board of Education, 1999)—both spare and concise models of clarity and purpose—to guide my teachers, rather than the 342-page *Principles and Standards for School Mathematics: Discussion Draft* (NCTM, 1998). Consider whether you would like to be held accountable for your students' mastering the following standards, then demonstrating that mastery in an assessment:

▶ Explore applications of other geometries in real-world contexts (New Jersey State Board of Education, 1997, p. 248).

▶ Use manipulatives, calculators, computers, and other tools, as appropriate, in order to strengthen mathematical thinking, understanding, and power to build on foundational concepts (Center for the Education and Study of Diverse Populations, undated, p. 1).

▶ Use sophisticated as well as basic problem-solving approaches to investigate, understand, and develop conjectures about mathematical concepts (Rhode Island Department of Education, 1996).

▶ Have students draw defensible inferences about unknown outcomes and make predictions, then identify the degree of confidence they have in their predictions (Michigan Department of Education, 1998).

▶ Create and use a variety of representations appropriately and with flexibility to organize, record, and communicate mathematical ideas (Oklahoma State Department of Education, 1999, p. 80).

In order to obtain complete commitment and unanimity among teachers, the curriculum must be worthy of their respect. If you and your staff are legally bound to uphold standards similar to the examples just cited, work with teachers to translate fuzzy standards into plain English so they have a readable road map for instruction.

## Concentrate on Collaborative Lesson Planning and Peer Observation

One of the more successful undertakings at my school during our improvement initiative was a program of peer observation. The teachers were initially reluctant about opening their classrooms to fellow teachers, but the Building Leadership team (a standing committee composed of rotating staff members that dealt with issues of instructional improvement and achievement) developed options for how classes could be observed (e.g., videotaping a class, then having the observed teacher watch the tape with a peer; the teacher to be observed inviting a peer of choice to observe; and for the more threatened teachers, simply watching a peer and discussing what was observed in his or her classroom). The Building Leadership team also helped structure the follow-up discussions in ways that allayed most of the teachers' fears. This program marked the beginning of a new openness among staff members. They came to understand that if we intended to increase student achievement, we had to connect our curriculum to ensure that all students were receiving the same content and quality of instruction. This meant collaborating with one another. If I were designing a similar program today, I would examine the Lesson Study Process as a possible model to adapt (Lewis & Tsuchida, 1998; Yoshida, 1999). My program would be designed by the faculty to reflect the culture of the American school and would cost far more than the program my Building Leadership team originally developed, but I am convinced that the achievement benefits would far outweigh any additional costs.

The Lesson Study Process as implemented in Japan is used by a group of same-grade-level teachers from one school who meet regularly throughout the school year to talk about instruction and to plan lessons using a process that has come to be fairly standardized across the country. It generally consists of eight steps (Yoshida, 1999):

1. Defining the problem

2. Planning the lesson

3. Teaching the lesson

4. Evaluating the lesson and reflecting on its effect

5. Revising the lesson

6. Teaching the revised lesson

7. Evaluating and reflecting again

8. Sharing the results

These eight steps generally focus on a single topic and lesson. This process is the centerpiece of any school improvement efforts in Japan (Lewis & Tsuchida, 1997; Lewis & Tsuchida, 1998; Shimahara, 1998; Shimahara & Sakai, 1995).

Yoshida (1999) spent one year with a primary-level lesson/study group in Hiroshima and reports his findings in an ethnographic study. Here are some of the topics that the group considered during their weeks of planning a lesson for the first unit on simple subtraction with the minuend larger than 10.

▶ The precise problem with which the lesson would begin, including such details as the exact terms to be used

▶ The manipulatives the students would be given to use in trying to solve the problem

▶ All the possible solutions, responses, and errors that students might produce as they tried to solve the problem

▶ The kinds of questions the teachers would ask to promote student thinking during the lesson and the kinds of direction/suggestion that could be given to students who showed one or another type of misconception in their thinking

▶ The organization of chalkboard space

▶ The allocation of available class time—45 minutes—to the various parts of the lesson

▶ Meeting the needs of individual students relative to their different levels of mathematical preparation

▶ Ending the lesson, considered a key moment for advancing students' understanding (pp. 82–146)

Many Japanese teachers videotape their research lessons, then show them to colleagues, asking them to give feedback on student behavior and student responses. While this type of activity can initially be stressful for those teachers who are accustomed to teaching in isolation, the benefits that accrue toward the improvement of instruction will outweigh the discomfort many teachers feel when teaching in front of their peers.

Some Japanese teachers open their research lessons to teachers from outside schools, sending invitations to neighboring districts. Imagine such an event in the United States. The closest I can come is a program we planned when I was a member of the Illinois Principals Association. I "volunteered" my sixth-grade teacher and her entire class of students to become a demonstration lesson for a group of more than a hundred principals. The teacher and her students traveled by bus to a nearby college campus, and we arranged her class in a large multipurpose area surrounded by circles of observers. The teacher taught a mathematics lesson for Part 1 of the demonstration, after which the students hopped on their bus to return to school with their parent chaperones and a student teacher. Part 2 featured three selected principals conferencing with the teacher as the group listened in. Then we opened up the discussion to everyone in the audience. The teacher responded graciously to any and all questions about what she had done and why. It was a powerful learning experience for everyone who attended—students, teacher, and principals.

*The Learning Essentials: Ways of Doing*

In addition to the three ways a school should be, there are a number of things that students must do in order to achieve excellence in mathematics.

*Early Numerical Abilities*

**What Do Children Know About Numbers When They Come to School and How Can We Do a Better Job of Building On That Knowledge?**

> "I have become increasingly impressed by young children's natural abilities to think about and use numbers and believe that these abilities should be given much greater recognition than they are at present. The fundamental question is how we can build on the talents and interests that children possess when they first start school, and so reduce the large number of children who leave school lacking both comprehension [of] and interest in mathematics."
>
> —Hughes, 1986, p. x

> "Think of informal mathematics as analogous to the child's spontaneous speech. Just as everyone learns to talk, and spoken language is the foundation for reading, so everyone develops an informal mathematics that should be the foundation for the written mathematics learned in school."
>
> —Ginsburg & Baron, 1993, p. 3

The knowledge young children have about mathematics and what they are able to do with mathematics has long fascinated researchers. One of the first and undeniably the most notable was Jean Piaget. Although Piaget's theories have had an enormous impact on mathematics instruction, his main interests actually lay in epistemology and psychology. However, his developmental stage theory has dominated the way in which many teachers have approached mathematics instruction in early childhood and primary education. Constance Kamii (1982, 1985) is one of his most ardent supporters, and her research on early childhood mathematics has been extraordinarily influential in convincing teachers that students are not capable of being taught math, but must discover it for themselves.

Piaget (1953) asserts that "it is a great mistake to suppose that a child acquires the notion of number and other mathematical concepts just from teaching. On the contrary, to a remarkable degree he develops them himself, independently and spontaneously. When adults try to impose mathematical concepts on a child prematurely, his learning is merely verbal; true understanding of them comes only with his mental growth" (p. 74). A child's capacity for learning is determined by his particular stage of development, Piaget theorized, and a child was not thought to be ready for a conceptual understanding of number until around the age of seven or eight (1952). Piaget's most commonly advanced "proof" of the young child's inability to understand arithmetic is the principle of *conservation*. According to Piaget, if a child cannot understand that when objects are moved around or put in different places, they remain the same in quantity, then the child doesn't understand the concept of number (Dehaene, 1997, p. 43).

Piaget laid the theoretical foundations for constructivism, the basis for many of our current mathematical approaches, by arguing that learning mathematics could not take place simply by the teacher transmitting knowledge to the learner. He argued that the building up of mathematical knowledge came about as a natural result of the more general growth of the child's logical capabilities. He emphasized that this "natural method of learning took place through the child's activities and through discovery" (1973, p. 85).

There were those who disagreed with Piaget, however. In 1954, Dantzig reiterated in the fourth edition of a book originally published in 1930 that "man, even in the lower stages of development, possesses a faculty which, for want of a better name, I shall call number sense. This faculty permits him to recognize that something has changed in a small collection when, without his direct knowledge, an object has been removed or added to the collection" (Dantzig, 1954, p. 1). Despite Dantzig's reassertion in 1954 of an inborn numerosity, Piaget's theories, especially conservation, would hold on for 20 more years before Piagetian constructivism was refuted and Dantzig's insights were indisputably substantiated.

Although we certainly cannot argue with Piaget's views that children need to understand what they are learning in the context of their own experiences and backgrounds, his theories have resulted in several widely held but badly misinformed instructional beliefs. The following is a summary of Piaget's views (Hughes, 1986, pp. 18–23) juxtaposed with various researchers' views of the real-life classroom.

1. *Piaget's View:* Teaching children before they are conceptually ready can produce only superficial learning—true learning comes only with the child's mental growth; to a large extent, mathematical concepts cannot be taught.

   *The Reality of the Classroom:* "Educators who use . . . direct approaches to mathematics teaching with children prior to the age of four or five are warned that their artificial structure and limitations serve only to lessen interest, exploration, and experimentation if those approaches are introduced before the child has experienced informal number activities. However, once the child has indicated an interest and need, and most will by the age of four or five, teachers can organize direct experiences with numbers that help children build desired concepts" (Maxim, 1989, p. 38).

2. *Piaget's View:* Learning mathematics is not essentially difficult, for it is something that children will, for the most part, do independently and spontaneously.

   *The Reality of the Classroom:* "Educators are in common agreement that the introduction of numeration concepts is the most difficult and important instruction task in mathematics in the early school years" (Resnick, 1983, p. 112).

3. *Piaget's View:* Children's understanding of conservation (i.e., the concept of the number of things irrespective of their position or size) determines their readiness to start on school arithmetic.

   *The Reality of the Classroom:* In day-care settings children as young as 24 to 35 months demonstrate an understanding of simple additions and subtractions (Starkey, 1983) and even spontaneously use strategies based on counting (Fuson, 1988).

4. *Piaget's View:* Teachers should mistrust any apparent ability—such as counting—that young children bring with them to school: If the children cannot conserve, then this apparent knowledge is likely to be merely parrot-style learning.

> *The Reality of the Classroom:* "Given that children's concepts are, in fact, far more sophisticated than has been traditionally assumed, it becomes all the more important to ensure that early education exploits the capabilities that young children have. At the same time, given the close link between early concepts and emerging theories, one of the central challenges is to help children overcome pervasive faulty theories, some of which appear to persist into adulthood" (Gelman, 1978 [Retrieved 1999 on-line]).

Believing that mathematics is not terribly difficult and that teachers are not responsible for designing instruction, many educators wait for students to bloom spontaneously, much like Leo did in the popular children's story *Leo, the Late Bloomer* (Lionni, 1971). Even though a growing number of developmental psychologists do not accept Piaget's conclusions about how children learn math, many teachers still cling to his theories when planning instruction for very young children.

Contrast Piaget's views to the increasing number of studies that demonstrate "infants as young as the first week of life do indeed categorize the world in terms of numerosities, and infants of a few weeks, too young to have learned about arithmetic, can add and subtract" (Butterworth, 1999, p. 99). Space does not permit describing all of the fascinating studies that support Butterworth's assertion, but his discussion of the numerical abilities of infants (pp. 97–147) as well as Geary's comprehensive treatment of the topic (1994, pp. 1–11) will change forever the way you think about a child's mathematical abilities.

Obviously children have a great deal of mathematical knowledge when they begin school. Why then do so many children have problems with school mathematics? Martin Hughes, a British researcher, was intrigued with this question and in *Children and Number: Difficulties in Learning Mathematics* (1986) he describes his quest for the answer. He explains for the benefit of his American readers that despite the pervasiveness of progressive education and constructivist methodologies in the British educational system, children there experience the same problems with grasping formal mathematics as students in this country who have experienced more traditional mathematics instruction. "If we had found that children possessed very few abilities on starting school, then perhaps their subsequent difficulty with school mathematics might be easier to accept. Instead we have something of a paradox. Young children appear to start school with more mathematical knowledge than has hitherto been thought. In that case why should they experience such difficulty with school mathematics?" (p. 36).

Hughes (1986) was fascinated with this conundrum and hypothesized that perhaps it was the new vocabulary of mathematics that was confounding so many children. But after additional research he determined that the problem seemed to have nothing to do with vocabulary and everything to do with whether children were adding and subtracting concrete objects. When they didn't have concrete objects to manipulate they had trouble. "Children start school at five years able to carry out simple additions and subtractions, provided these take place in contexts involving specific objects, people, or events. In contrast, when they are presented with similar additions and subtractions in contexts where there is no reference to specific objects [e.g., 2 + 2 = ], they are usually unable to answer" (p. 39).

Additional research with small groups of children brought Hughes (1986) closer to an understanding of what he perceived to be the real problem. It was not the concepts of addition and subtraction that were at the heart of the difficulty. Students clearly understood them, as demonstrated by their ability to perform the operations with concrete representations. Nor did they seem to need additional hands-on experiences with manipulatives. Rather, he determined, it was the symbols used to represent the concepts of addition and subtraction that were causing the problem. Hughes hypothesizes that the formal code of mathematics is much like a secret code: It is completely context free and rests heavily on written symbolism. Both the written and the context-free natures of this formal code cause considerable difficulties for young children in spite of the range of mathematical abilities with which they start school.

Hughes (1986) suggests that we have two important tasks as educators: to help children learn this symbolic language and to assist them in learning to translate back and forth between the concrete and symbolic languages. "The concept of translation thus provides an important way of thinking about mathematical understanding. . . . Children need to be able to translate a formal problem into a concrete representation or to translate a concrete representation into a formal problem. They need the ability to go back and forth between these two languages. Many of the difficulties which children have with mathematical problems in the classroom are closely related to problems in translating between the formal and the concrete" (p. 170).

Older students seem to have their own set of translation problems. Having finally mastered the symbolic language, they then find it difficult to translate going in the opposite direction: from a concrete "story problem" into a formal problem. Rathmell (1975) found that when pupils were given numerals appropriate to their grade level (e.g., two-digit numerals for second-graders, decimals for sixth-graders), most could write them, read them, and represent them with manipulative models. However, many had difficulty with translating the numerals to expanded notation and with regrouping, estimating, and solving problems involving such numbers.

Teachers must find ways to help children connect the mathematical concepts and skills they already possess with the symbols and rules that are part of the mathematics that is taught in school. Many children will not make this connection unless it is systematically taught to them. Hughes (1986) further points out that this emphasis on the difficult nature of learning mathematics makes a strong and important contrast with Piaget's argument that mathematical concepts occur naturally and spontaneously. Hughes suggests that we must continually explain the history and purpose of conventional symbolism and that we should be as explicit as possible in explaining to children what the symbols are called, what they look like, and, most important, why they are used.

### The Big Ideas in Early Mathematical Learning

1. *Before* beginning instruction, find out as much as possible about a child's mathematical background and what the child already knows. The Number Knowledge Test (Griffin, Case, & Siegler, 1994, p. 30) is an excellent instrument for identifying students at risk of mathematics failure because of their lack of conceptual knowledge regarding number. Make no assumptions. Most children have two types of mathematics learning when they begin formal schooling: (a) patterns of thought and perception

for dealing with quantitative problems (addition and subtraction,) which occur spontaneously, and (b) counting, which is a culturally transmitted skill (Ginsburg, 1989). There are children, however, who, because of a possible mathematics disability or lack of early experiences with math, will need intense direct and systematic instruction to prepare them for success in math learning.

2. Emphasize both the concrete and the symbolic in early instruction. They are equally important, and having just one, irrespective of which one it is, will put a child at a serious disadvantage. Find ways to help children learn how to skillfully translate in either direction by providing excellent instruction and constant opportunities for practice.

3. Build on the strategies children already use. When children have figured out something on their own, use that information to extend their learning.

4. Just as children invent spelling, they also invent symbolism for numerical operations. Respect children's invented symbolism. Work with children's own representations of addition and subtraction before introducing them to the conventional plus and minus sign.

## The Concept of Numeration

### The Critical Importance of Numeration As a Basis for Mathematical Learning

Mathematical ideas are like building blocks; it is generally accepted that more complex mathematical ideas build on simpler ones. Without a thorough understanding of the concept of numeration (i.e., the base-10 place value system), a student will be unable to succeed in mathematics. The instructional decisions teachers make relative to the teaching and learning of numeration may well set a child on the road to mathematical success or ensure confusion and even math-phobia.

> "Many of the difficulties children have in arithmetic result from not understanding number ideas supposedly learned at an earlier time."
> —Engelhardt, Ashlock, & Wiebe, 1984, p. 12

There are a variety of studies to support the idea that American children have substantial difficulties with numeration (Diens, 1970; Good, 1979). A great many of the problems that American students have with place value can undoubtedly be attributed to English number words. Many Asian languages use number words in which the place value is inherent in the words. For example, the Chinese word for "1" is *yi*, the word for "2" is *er*, and the word for "10" is *shi*. "11" is *shi yi*. "12" is *shi er*. This principal of additive composition in Asian languages makes place value much easier to understand and results in earlier fluent arithmetic skills for Asian children (Miller & Stigler, 1987).

A second reason many American children may have difficulty with place value is that their teachers do not understand the concept. In *Knowing and Teaching Elementary Mathematics,* Liping Ma (1999) describes interviews with U.S. and Chinese teachers regarding how they would deal with students' mistakes in multidigit multiplications in which the students seemed to be forgetting to "move the numbers" (i.e., the partial products) over on each line. The students were making this common error:

```
      123
   x 645
      615
      492
      738
     1845
```

instead of doing it correctly, like this:

```
      123
   x 645
      615
      492
      738
    79335
```

Seventy percent of the American teachers thought that the mistake students were making was simply a matter of the lining-up procedure. One teacher strongly stated how important understanding was and that it should precede memorization, explaining that she would have students put zeros in so that they could line up the numbers correctly; however, the teacher was unable to provide a mathematically legitimate explanation for why including the zeros makes sense (Ma, 1999, p. 37). When other American teachers in the sample were asked whether placing zeros in the problem might help their students, the confused teachers saw the zeros in a variety of ways: useful placeholders, alien to the computation, artificial, and not even belonging in the problem (p. 32). More than 60% of the U.S. teachers Ma interviewed were unable to provide authentic conceptual explanations for the procedure while more than 90% of the Chinese teachers were able to present a conceptual basis (p. 52).

A thorough understanding of the base-10 system is important for three reasons (Geary, 1994, pp. 44–46). First, students cannot grasp the conceptual meaning of spoken and written multidigit numbers without a thorough understanding of the base-10 system.

Second, understanding that multidigit numbers represent groups of 100s, 10s, and 1s influences the sophistication of the problem-solving strategies the student can use to solve complex arithmetic problems.

And, finally, understanding the base-10 system is important in order to be able to regroup and figure out place value. Fuson (1988) recommends that kindergarten children learn basic word names and be introduced to the base-10 system. Since number words are arbitrary, simply hearing the sounds associated with the words offers no clues about their meaning. So even children who understand that counting and quantity are related—and Gelman and Gallistel believe that is innate—may have to memorize number names (Gelman & Gallistel, 1978).

### The Big Ideas in Numeration

1. Understanding the base-10 system and place value are absolutely essential mathematical learnings.

2. Students should be carefully and thoughtfully introduced to place value in kindergarten. Kindergarten teachers could well use the development of an introductory place value lesson as their first project for a research lesson. Readings that might inform the teachers' discussion and planning include Fuson (1988) and Gelman & Gallistel (1978).

3. Students should learn the number names and be able to count to 30 by the end of kindergarten.

4. Students who are having difficulties in mathematics in upper grades should be assessed both formally with a paper and pencil test and informally through interview and observation for their understanding of place value to determine if remediation is necessary. Every teacher should read *Knowing and Teaching Elementary Mathematics* (Ma, 1999).

## Reading and Language Development

### Reading and Language Development: Prerequisites for Success in Mathematics

Until recently, scientists could only speculate about how the human brain actually did math. Some theorists believed that language was a crucial aspect of mathematics, and others, Albert Einstein, for example, said it was not (Blakeslee, 1999 [On-line]). Now Stanislas Dehaene and his colleagues (Dehaene, Spelke, Pinel, Stanescu, & Tsivkin, 1999) have used brain imaging techniques to identify two circuits in the brain, one that handles giving names to numbers, carrying out exact calculations, and storing arithmetic knowledge like multiplication facts and another that is used for estimating quantities and other numerical relationships. Dehaene et al. hypothesize that the first circuit is language based and that the second one is rather like a mental number line and is used to approximate and manipulate quantities. The language-mathematics connection is a strong one.

School officials in Sacramento, California, have seen the power of the language-mathematics connection firsthand. Educators there have been engaged in a massive reading improvement initiative for two and a half years. When the results of the Stanford 9 Test were posted in June 1999, all concerned were delighted to note that mathematics achievement had also risen (Kollars, 1999 [On-line]). This is not surprising, given the important role that vocabulary, language development, and reading comprehension play in mathematics achievement. No longer can content-area teachers, especially mathematics teachers, ignore their role as reading teachers. Once children have learned to read, they also need to be taught how to read to learn. These are different skills, both for the learner and the teacher—especially in mathematics. Classroom and subject-matter teachers must provide simultaneous instruction in reading skills along with instruction in course content. Ebeling (1974) found, for example, that "the average sixth-grade student has the ability to associate fewer than half of the algorithms with their mathematical terms" (p. 7515).

Vocabulary and reading deficiencies are most likely to influence mathematics achievement in the area of problem solving. It comes as no surprise to learn that reading skill is related to success with problem solving (Balow, 1964). Here are some reading strategies that mathematics teachers might build into lessons, particularly those that involve problem solving (Creative Publications, 1978, pp. 153–154).

◆ Teach students that a single reading of a word problem is often not enough. Three readings may actually not be too many for some students and for some problems. Ask students to paraphrase the word problem before beginning to work on the solution.

◆ Encourage students to use graphic organizers, such as diagrams, figures, sketches, and flow charts, to help them with problem solving.

◆ Help students who have reading difficulties to make the transition to more difficult word problems by first giving them problems with shorter sentences, easier vocabulary, and an accompanying diagram or graphic organizer.

◆ Ask students to write their own story problems. Group several students, assign the task of writing several story problems, then ask them to solve each other's problems.

◆ Practice translation activities. For example, give an equation and have students write a word problem to illustrate it. Or give students a simple story problem and ask them to write the equation. This activity can be done from kindergarten through 12th grade.

◆ Expose students to story problems that give insufficient information, too much information, or hidden information (e.g., price per pound is given but students need to compute price per ounce). These kinds of problems force students to read more carefully for understanding.

### The Big Ideas in Reading and Language Development As They Influence Mathematics Achievement

1. When students are failing mathematics, assess their reading level using fiction, expository text, and mathematical problems.

2. Expect all mathematics teachers to be alert for ways in which they can help students become more competent readers of mathematics.

3. Preview and discuss difficult vocabulary. Do not assume that students know the meanings of mathematical terms.

4. Regularly ask students (or small groups of students) to explain a concept, an algorithm, or a problem-solving method. According to Stevenson and Stigler (1992, p. 37), Japanese teachers spend more time than American teachers in encouraging their students to produce comprehensive verbal explanations of mathematical concepts and algorithms. This may contribute to Japanese children's success in mathematics.

## Arithmetic Facts and Algorithms

### How Important Are Arithmetic Facts and Algorithms and What Is the Role of Practice in Learning Them?

In a relatively recent article on teaching the value of coins to primary students, the authors make two statements: "Many teachers try to use memorization techniques for teaching monetary objectives related to value. Memorization, however, is a poor method of teaching or learning" (Drum & Petty, 1999, p. 264). The authors go on to support their statements using the recommendations from the NCTM 1989 Standards regarding the deemphasis on rote memory as a teaching and learning technique (NCTM, 1989, pp. 21, 73). No educator would ever argue that conceptual understanding isn't critical and shouldn't be a foremost goal of our teaching, but painting memory with such a broad brush as to label it a "poor method" causes one to wonder if these gentlemen have ever taken music lessons, learned to read, or played a sport. "In order to play a flute sonata fluently you have to break it apart and practice several measures over and over again until eventually your fingers can fly over the notes almost automatically. Overlearning and repeated exposure leads to automaticity, just as practice with phrases and patterns leads to automaticity in reading words" (Hall & Moats, 1998, p. 140). The same principle applies to mathematics learning. Automaticity and fluency free up working memory so that students can concentrate on interpretation and metacognition, whether the task is playing a sonata, reading a book, or solving a problem.

> "We must conclude that the most effective device that can be applied to learning is to increase the amount of drill or practice. No devices offer more hope for increasing learning than those which give each individual pupil more opportunity to practice."
> —Symonds & Chase, 1929, p. 34
>
> "[A] deep understanding of mathematics ultimately lies within the skills."
> —Wu, 1999, p. 51

There are many occasions when students understand the concepts very well (e.g., students who understand counting intuitively) and merely need to store some information in their memory banks (e.g., the names of number words) to free up their working memory for doing other things. Geary (1994) discusses two kinds of competencies that need to be present not only in arithmetic, discussed here, but in mathematical problem solving discussed later: conceptual and procedural (p. 269). Conceptual understanding is of primary concern when a child is learning about place value, for example. "Procedural skills, on the other hand, are associated with the use of specific algorithms or equations for solving arithmetic or mathematics problems. Not only are conceptual and procedural competencies different, they require different forms of instruction" (Cooper & Sweller, 1987; Novick, 1992). "Procedural learning requires extensive practice on a wide variety of problems on which the procedure might eventually be used" (Geary, 1994, p. 269). Although procedural learning has fallen on hard times since the NCTM Standards were published in 1989 and is considered unnecessary by many constructivists (Cobb et al., 1992), it remains a critical component of raising mathematics achievement. The automaticity that results from quality practice has the potential to free up students' attention and working memory so they can concentrate on other features of a problem (Geary & Widaman, 1992; NCTM Research Advisory Committee, 1988).

Not only do the current mathematical reforms deemphasize memory and practice generally, they specifically recommend decreased attention to mastery of the long division algorithm, paper-and-pencil fraction computation, teaching computations out of context, and drilling on paper and pencil algorithms (NCTM, 1989, pp. 21, 73).

There are those who are even ready to completely abandon computational algorithms. They believe that "drill and practice of computational algorithms devour an incredibly large proportion of instructional time, precluding any real chance for actually applying mathematics and developing the conceptual understanding that underlies mathematical literacy" (Leinwand, February 9, 1994 [On-line]).

But before we end our "obsessive love affair with pencil-and-paper computation," as Leinwand (1994) characterizes it, ponder whether the students who struggle with computational algorithms because of lack of automaticity will really fare any better with calculators. Since "algorithmic thinking provides the formal structure for mathematical growth and understanding" (Mingus & Grassl, 1998, p. 32) and it is understanding that is critical to solving the problem, these students may continue to flounder even with a calculator crutch.

There are two aspects of arithmetic that receive most of the criticism with regard to "drill and kill": basic math facts and algorithms. Frankly, it is difficult to conceive of skill and fluency in problem solving without mastery of these two aspects of arithmetic. Basic math facts are a prerequisite for solving even simple word problems (Wu, 1999), and mastery of the algorithms that manipulate those facts is even more critical. Conversely, a curriculum that stresses only the memorization and drill of the facts and the algorithms without daily solving of challenging word problems is as destitute as one that omits them completely. Both are necessary. Facts and algorithms are the tools of problem solving. If a student cannot master the facts and algorithms, it is not likely that the presence of a calculator will suddenly bestow problem-solving abilities on a student. Calculators give power, but it is not a magical power.

Exactly what are these critical facts and algorithms? There are 390 basic arithmetic facts, and once a skilled teacher is finished with lessons and activities that build an understanding of the concept of multiplication and has then helped students see how the various facts relate to one another in families, all that remains is mastery (Stein, et al., 1997, pp. 79–93). My son, Patrick, had the "understanding" and "relating" aspects of multiplication down cold. He could explain, conceptualize, and demonstrate with manipulatives ad nauseum, but his fourth-grade teacher also demanded mastery, an idea he found unattractive. So we went to work with good old-fashioned drill and practice. A few flash cards, some threats, and a reward or two and the job was done. I have found that lack of mastery is more often a dearth of will and motivation than a lack of ability. Patrick's M.A. in economics and Ph.D. in international comparative education are certainly all the evidence I need that drill didn't kill his motivation for higher mathematics!

"An algorithm is a precise, systematic method for solving a class of problems. An algorithm takes input, follows a determinate set of rules, and, in a finite number of steps, gives output that provides a conclusive answer" (Maurer, 1998, 21). Algorithms are efficient and tidy. Is there often more than one way to arrive at an answer? Of course. Is it wrong if students choose to invent their own algorithm? Of course not. Is the teaching of algorithms to students an end itself? Never. The purpose of learning algorithms is to facilitate fluent and accurate problem solving, not to be able to regurgitate formulas. In fact, when students are practicing simple problems using the mastered algorithm, they often develop additional insights and strategies they are unaware of using (Siegler & Stern, 1998).

The Grade One Standards for the State of California offer an excellent example of the balance and unity that must exist between conceptual and procedural understandings for students to develop into well-rounded mathematicians. Students are expected to "understand and use the concept of 1s and 10s in the place value number system, add and subtract small numbers with ease, measure with simple units and locate objects in space, and describe data and analyze and solve simple problems" (California State Board of Education, 1999, p. 4).

### The Big Ideas in the Mastery of Basic Facts and Algorithms

1. Students should be expected to memorize math facts at some agreed-upon point in their school careers. If they are not expected to do so, they won't! This might be a possible timetable (California State Board of Education, 1999, pp. 4, 8, 11):

   a. Addition facts (sums to 20) and the corresponding subtraction facts memorized by the end of first grade

   b. Multiplication tables of 2s, 5s, and 10s (to 10 x 10) memorized by the end of second grade

   c. The remainder of the multiplication tables memorized (all numbers between 1 and 10) by the end of third grade

2. Students should be expected to master the standard algorithms for addition, subtraction, multiplication, and division of whole numbers at some agreed-upon point in their school careers. This might be a possible timetable (California State Board of Education, 1999, pp. 16, 21).

   a. Standard algorithms for the addition and subtraction of multidigit numbers by end of fourth grade

   b. Standard algorithms for multiplying a multidigit number by a two-digit number and for dividing a multidigit number by a one-digit number by the end of fourth grade

   c. Standard algorithm for long division with multidigit divisors by the end of fifth grade

## Mathematical Problem Solving

### What Is Problem Solving and How Can We Cultivate Students' Ability to Do It?

> "Learning to problem solve is an essential feature of children's mathematical development, but unfortunately it is a skill that most children in the United States apparently do not master."
> —Geary, 1994, p. 95

The issue of problem solving and how students at every grade level can become skilled mathematical problem solvers is a critical one to raising mathematics achievement. "Mathematics is only 'useful' to the extent which it can be applied to a particular situation, and it is the ability to apply mathematics to a variety of situations to which we give the name 'problem solving.' However, the solution of a mathematical problem cannot begin until the problem has been translated into the appropriate mathematical terms. This first and essential step presents very great difficulties to many pupils—a fact which is often too little appreciated" (Cockcroft, 1982). How do students learn this critical translation skill? Most students apparently cannot construct it for themselves or problem-solving scores in the United States would not be so abysmal. Expecting children to develop their own problem-solving model is a bit like teaching them to swim by pushing them off the high dive and cheering them on from the sidelines as they attempt to construct their own technique for getting back to the ladder. Of course, some will figure out how to do it, but the majority will drown. Students learn problem solving best when lessons are designed around well-chosen problems, when varying solutions are explored and evaluated, and when errors are not considered mistakes, but rather opportunities for learning. Students become skilled problem solvers in the same way that students become good readers—by doing a lot of it. But like reading a lot, solving a lot must be done at an ever-increasing level of difficulty and with a relentless constancy. Remember the third grade Russian textbook with its 1,091 word problems that we mentioned earlier in the book? Imagine how skilled those Russian students will become in problem solving after they have discussed and digested an average of more than five challenging problems every day.

What is problem solving? "Problem solving may be thought of as the process of applying previously learned rules and understandings to a situation which, for the learner, is new and different. When considering mathematics, the most common means for portraying problem-solving situations are through the use of word problems. These *story problems,* as they are often called, provide a bridge from the basic arithmetic skills of the primary grades to the application of such skills in real-world settings (Briars & Larkin, 1984).

The question of whether problem solving should be discovered or taught has received a great deal of discussion during the tenure of the NCTM 1989 Standards. Although the authors of that document asserted that problem solving should be the central focus of the mathematics curriculum (p. 23) and that "in its broadest sense, it is nearly synonymous with doing mathematics" (p. 137), the ways in which students would eventually make the quantum leap from novice to expert problem solvers was never really spelled out. An important goal for instruction in the standards was to enable children to develop and apply a variety of strategies to solve problems (p. 24), but there is no mention made of the need for students to be instructed in when and how to use these strategies or how development of the strategies would occur spontaneously through discovery.

The revised NCTM standards to be published in 2000 include a definite shift in position on whether problem solving should be discovered or taught, a point of contention in the 1989 Standards. Unfortunately, the authors of the draft copy of the revised standards delay their unequivocal commitment to instruction of problem solving until Grades 9 through 12: "Problem-solving activity must be embedded in the fabric of students' mathematics learning. Equally important is the finding that if strategies are not taught explicitly, students are not likely to learn them. Problem-solving strategies are complex and subtle, and students cannot be expected to pick them up by osmosis" (NCTM, 1998, October, p. 315). One has to read nearly the entire document to find this extraordinarily important statement, however. The discussion regarding problem solving in prekindergarten through second grade presents a very different view. "Problem solving is natural to small children, for whom much of the world is new and whose responses are often unconstrained by previous habit. The challenge in prekindergarten, kindergarten, and Grades 1 and 2 is to help children's innate problem-solving inclinations *develop* [italics added] so that they have a positive problem-solving disposition, develop and use a variety of problem-solving strategies, and incorporate habits of monitoring and adjusting" (NCTM, 1998, p. 134). There is no discussion regarding problem-solving instruction in the prekindergarten through second-grade levels at all, although teachers *are* encouraged to "call attention to the strategies students and their classmates are using" (p. 136). The recommendation for third through fifth grades regarding problem solving doesn't even suggest that teachers showcase the strategies that are discovered by students. Rather, "the teacher's role in helping students become problem solvers is to establish the classroom environment, select rich and appropriate tasks or problems, orchestrate their use, and assess students' understanding. Critical to the development of confident, self-assured problem solvers are the social norms established in the classroom by the teacher. Students must be taught to respect and value one another's ideas and ways of thinking" (pp. 188–189). The emphasis seems to shift at Grades 3 through 5 to problem solving in groups, and there are no statements such as the one found in the discussion about Grades 9 through 12 relative to the importance of teaching the strategies to students.

Instruction *is* mentioned in the discussion about Grades 6 through 8 as one way to help students become more skilled at problem solving. "Although it is not the main focus of problem solving in the middle grades, when students learn *about* problem solving they become familiarized with a number of problem-solving heuristics [problem solving strategies or methodologies], such as looking for patterns, solving a simpler problem, making a table, and working backwards. These are general strategies that are useful when no known approach to a problem is readily at hand. Many of these heuristics will already have been widely used in the elementary grades, but middle-grade students need additional experience and instruction in which they consider how to use those strategies appropriately and effectively" (NCTM, 1998, p. 246). Only one conclusion can be drawn from this somewhat schizophrenic treatment of an extraordinarily important issue: at least three, possibly four, different groups of individuals wrote the four grade-level sections on problem solving, and they failed to align this issue throughout the document.

### The Big Ideas in Problem Solving

1. Students must be able to read with comprehension and understanding to solve written problems in mathematics. Problem solving isn't always about mathematics. Sometimes it's about reading. There are several important semantic aspects of problem solving (DeCorte & Verschaffel, 1991):

   a. Word problems that can be solved by the same arithmetic operation but differ with respect to underlying semantic structure have very different degrees of difficulty.

   b. The degree to which the underlying semantic structure is made explicit in a problem's text affects the degree of difficulty of a problem.

   c. The order in which numbers are presented in a problem affects the degree of difficulty.

2. Students must understand and have internalized a problem-solving model similar to the one that follows. The first statement in each step comes from my independently conceived problem-solving model. The quotes that follow each statement are from DeCorte and Verschaffel's model (1991, p. 118).

a. Students must be able to read and understand the problem. "A complex goal-oriented, text-processing activity occurs; starting from the verbal text, the pupil constructs a global, abstract, internal representation of the problem in terms of sets and set relations."

b. Students must then be able to translate what they have read into mathematical symbols. "On the basis of that representation, the problem solver selects an appropriate formal arithmetic operation or an informal counting strategy to find the unknown element in the problem representation."

c. Students must then be able to solve (either by hand or with a calculator) for the correct answer to the problem. "The selected action or operation is executed."

d. Finally, students must be able to translate the answer back into the context of the problem. "The problem solver reactivates the initial problem representation, replaces the unknown element by the result of the action performed, and formulates the answer."

3. Problem-solving abilities of the type seen in the students of many Asian countries, particularly Japan, can only be taught through daily lessons focused on well-chosen problems.

4. Choosing the right problems to present to students for solution at various points along their problem-solving journey is extraordinarily important.

5. In order for students to become skilled problem solvers they must solve many different kinds of problems. Errors should be seen as opportunities for learning. Individual differences among students should be viewed as a resource for the class because "they produce a range of ideas and solution methods that provide the material for students' discussion and reflection" (Stigler & Hiebert, 1999, p. 94).

## *Algebra*

### How Important Is Algebra?

The only thing that almost everyone seems to agree on is that algebra is important. It has been called the gateway course to more rigorous math and science classes and there is no question that it definitely opens doors for students. Related issues are still being debated, however. Should every student be required to take algebra? Or is it a waste of time if you're never going to be a scientist or mathematician? Further, how should algebra be taught? As a separate class or integrated with many other mathematics topics? And when should we teach it? In eighth grade, ninth grade, or over all three years of middle school?

The NCTM 1989 Standards called for informal explorations of algebraic concepts in fifth- through eighth-grade curricula, rather than the inclusion of an eighth-grade algebra course per se

> "Algebra is the language through which most of mathematics is communicated."
> —NCTM, 1989, p. 150
>
> ———<◇>———
>
> "It seems likely [given the U.S. tradition for lowering expectations, covering many simple topics, and repackaging content in less demanding form] that if all eighth graders were to take algebra, algebra would become such that all eighth graders could take it."
> —Schmidt et al., 1999, p. 208

(NCTM, 1989, pp. 102–104). Many policy makers are calling for a mandated eighth-grade algebra course, citing our poor eighth-grade performance on the TIMSS as compared to other countries (U.S. Department of Education, 1997).

> "Mathematics is the language of science, and algebra is the minimum vocabulary that scientists of every discipline use to describe their work."
> —Castro, 1997, p. 16

> "Let's face it. For most students the current school approach to algebra is an unmitigated disaster. One out of every four students never takes algebra, being diverted instead into dead-end sidings such as general or consumer mathematics. And half the students who do take first-year algebra leave the course with a lifelong distaste for mathematics."
> —Steen, 1992, 258

Edward Silver, professor of mathematics at the University of Pittsburgh, disagrees. He believes that "mandating an algebra course at Grade 8 for all students is likely to focus attention on algebraic ideas in one year rather than blend algebraic thinking and skills across three years of middle-grade mathematics" (Silver, 1997, p. 205). Are students better off with a salt-and-pepper approach to algebra or with a self-contained course in which the content is systematically and explicitly taught in a sequential manner? There are strong opinions on both sides. Whatever we do, we must do something differently. The current middle school curriculum as described in the TIMSS data lacks intellectual rigor. In fact, the topics covered in the United States' seventh- and eighth-grade classrooms are much like those covered in third and fourth grades—lots of arithmetic (Schmidt et al., 1999, p. 49). In Japan and Korea, arithmetic is taught for mastery in those early grades and students then move on to a more algebra- and geometry-centered curriculum. One of the most disappointing aspects of the TIMSS report as it described the United States was what a small amount of new learning actually occurred during the eighth grade. Since both seventh- and eighth-graders took the same test, researchers had the unique opportunity of creating a quasi-longitudinal study. Sadly, there was no significant difference between the scores of U.S. students at the end of seventh and eighth grades.

When students fail to succeed in a given course of study, it is all too easy to blame the course. But the problem might also be the result of inadequate preparation and poor foundational learnings on the part of the students or low expectations for students. To succeed in algebra a student needs to be competent in ordinary fraction arithmetic and comfortable with simple symbolic representation (W. Bishop, personal communication, February 9, 2000). Students have difficulty with algebra for one of the same reasons they have difficulty with arithmetic—an inability to translate word problems into mathematical symbols (equations) that they can solve. Algebraic translating involves assigning variables, noting constants, and representing relationships among variables (Mayer, 1982). Translating algebraic word problems into equations is similar to translating word problems into simple arithmetic problems, with the added advantage that algebraic notation can handle more complicated data and problems that seem impossible become easy.

Although the body of research into how students develop automaticity and skill in algebraic problem solving is not as well developed as the research into arithmetical problem solving, some key points emerge:

► Students need good reading skills, a sufficient amount of working memory, and basic computational skills to be successful in algebra.

► Students need rule automation, that is, ease with basic algebraic procedures such as subtracting and adding variables to each side of an equation and being able to automatically execute a procedure without having to think about the rules governing the procedure (Cooper & Sweller, 1987).

▶ Students need metacognition, the ability to think about the problems they are solving apart from actually solving them, then choose the most efficient way to solve the problem. Metacognition develops from extensive experience in solving similar problems (Bransford & the Cognition and Technology Group of Vanderbilt University, 1993). "With experience, people presumably figure out which approaches work and which do not work for solving problems in the same category" (Geary, 1994, p. 126).

The above discussion points to the way in which I want students in my fantasy school to become proficient in algebra: solving a lot of problems. Practice, practice, practice. "Symbolic reasoning and calculations with symbols are central in algebra. Through the study of algebra, a student develops an understanding of the symbolic language of mathematics and the sciences. In addition, algebraic skills and concepts are developed and used in a wide variety of problem-solving situations (California State Board of Education, 1999, p. 38).

One of my favorite algebra teachers is Carol Gambill. She taught at the Sewickley Academy in the Pittsburgh area for many years and is now chair of the mathematics department and vice principal of the Littleton, Colorado, Prep Charter School. Carol has developed what her students call the "Gambill Method." I would hire Carol to teach algebra at my fantasy school in a heartbeat if I could. Here is the Gambill Method described in Carol's own words. Compare it to the way your students are learning algebra.

"Most students who enter my eighth-grade Algebra I or Honors Algebra I classes in September each year are ill-prepared to learn algebra because most of them have not fully mastered arithmetic. To make matters worse, I have too few class periods to teach them the entire rigorous course when one adds up the drug education activities, annual class trips, report card day, vacations, snow days, exams, and parent-teacher conferences. These restrictions demand that the students put in extensive quality time outside of class grappling with difficult problems and practicing for accuracy.

"I devised a method that I have used for 15 years with all students, those with disabilities, the average student, and those who are gifted. This method really works. Students make incredible gains during their year with me, because of the system the kids long ago dubbed the Gambill Method. Here's how it works.

"Twenty to thirty problems are assigned for homework every evening, ranging from the easiest to the most difficult of a given section of the text. I always assign the odd problems because their answers are in the back of the book. The answers provide the students with road maps to mastery. If they don't get the correct answer it means they turn back, take a detour, change a flat tire, or find a service station.

"On the day that an assignment is given I do the even problems with students in class using direct instruction. Although I use a traditional algebra textbook (Brown, Dolciani, & Sorgenfrey, 1994), I have developed totally scripted lessons for each algebra unit that require absolute focus and attention, constant oral responses, and intense involvement from every student. Direct instruction assures that all students leave my classroom that day with a thorough understanding and at least partial mastery of the concepts. I tell my students that doing homework does not merely mean writing out the problems, although that most assuredly is a component. I tell them they must master completely every problem of the assignment from the easiest to the most difficult. I would never assign a problem for which I had not given them the answer. The next day when the students walk in the door I give them their daily quiz over the most difficult four or five problems from that assignment. Their answers and all of their work toward that end must be accurate. Some students work more quickly than others; the first students finished come up and have their papers checked by me, then they become student checkers and grade recorders, and so it progresses, with more and more checkers becoming available as the slower students finish their daily quizzes.

"Within 15 minutes, all students in the class have taken a daily quiz over the previous night's homework assignment. The quizzes have been graded and recorded and are back in the students' hands, thus providing daily immediate feedback to each student on his or her own progression toward mastery, and providing me, of course, with instant knowledge as to whether or not students did their homework.

"I never ask to see the homework of any student unless that student has failed the daily quiz. If I ask to see the homework of a student who has failed, and the student does not have it, he gets an immediate detention for the day. A detention simply means that students must stay after school that day and do under school supervision the assignment that they failed to do on their own. This, in my opinion, is a justifiable, logical consequence.

"Because I am so strict with mastery of homework concepts, I assure the students that I will also do my part to help them be successful. Therefore, I conduct extra help sessions before school and at both lunch periods. It is gratifying to see five to ten eighth-graders gathered around my chalkboard before school, excitedly discussing a difficult algebra problem. The kids love these chalkboard algebra debate sessions. In addition, the students have my telephone number and are invited to call me as a last resort. Please note, however, that I seldom receive more than two calls per school year.

"My students win so many academic awards that students from other algebra classes cannot even play in their league. There is much hard work and yet the students love my class, vote it their favorite each year, love math (even those who had despised it up until algebra) and remember their year with me as the one that led them to discover within themselves the power to determine their own destiny in the academic arena. All this is based on a simple system that nurtures and demands daily perfect mastery of each step in the course as it comes along. Other teachers who have adopted the Gambill Method have replicated my results" (Carol Gambill, personal communication, August 13, 1999).

One of the reasons I want Carol to teach math in my fantasy school is that she achieves remarkable success with her students. They have repeatedly won a variety of mathematics competition championships at the local, state, and national levels for the past 10 years. They took first place in the Pittsburgh MathCounts Competition for five consecutive years and won a Pennsylvania State MathCounts championship as well. And based on the outstanding achievements of Carol's students on the American Junior High School Math Exam, the NCTM presented her with the Edith Mae Sliffe Award. But awards are not the only or even the most important reason for my wanting Carol to teach in my school. Most important to me is that her students know exactly what is expected of them, and Carol is disciplined and structured enough to be consistent.

There are several things that educators, policy makers, and community members can do to ensure that all students experience equity and quality with regard to algebra instruction:

▶ Provide all students in the eighth grade with the opportunity to take algebra I or a similarly demanding course that includes fundamental algebraic concepts.

▶ Build the groundwork for success in algebra by providing rigorous curriculum in kindergarten through seventh grade that moves beyond arithmetic and prepares students for the transition to algebra.

▶ Ensure that students, parents, teachers, and counselors understand the importance of students' early study of algebra as well as their continued study of rigorous mathematics and science in high school (U.S. Department of Education, 1997, p. 28).

**The Big Ideas in Algebra**

1. Prepare students for algebra with a rigorous curriculum for kindergarten through seventh grade.

2. Provide algebra for as many students as you possibly can. Offer a course in both eighth and ninth grades to increase the likelihood that more students will have the opportunity to master algebra.

3. Offer a prealgebra course in eighth grade for those students who need additional preparation and a slower instructional pace.

> "Lack of understanding leads to confusion, confusion to anxiety, avoidance, and no further learning. For people to enjoy mathematical activities, understanding is the key."
> —Butterworth, 1999, p. 317

## High School Mathematics

### What Is the Purpose of High School Math and How Much Is Enough?

What should be the purpose of high school mathematics? The eminent French mathematician Jean Dieudonne put it well: "For what good do we seek? Certainly it is not to introduce them [students] to collections of more or less ingenious theorems about the bisectors of the angles of a triangle or the sequence of prime numbers, but rather to teach them to order and link their thoughts according to the methods mathematicians use, because we recognize in this exercise a way to develop a clear mind and excellent judgment. It is the mathematical method that ought to be the object of our teaching, the subject matter being only well-chosen illustrations of it."

High school mathematics has traditionally been organized around courses that progressed in a somewhat predictable way. As more math programs based on the NCTM Standards have been developed, this tradition is less likely to be followed. Programs such as *College Preparatory Mathematics* (a three-year sequence that integrates algebra, geometry, and trigonometry) and *Interactive Mathematics Program* (a four-year curriculum of problem-based, integrated mathematics designed to replace the traditional algebra I–geometry–algebra II/trigonometry–precalculus sequence) integrate the usual traditional math courses over a period of three to four years. These programs focus on technology and NCTM-based recommendations and are problem based. For example, in *Interactive Mathematics Program* most units begin with a central problem that students explore over the course of six to eight weeks (Reed, 1999, pp. 192–196). This kind of total problem-based study without a well-defined concurrent strand of specific and explicit content is controversial and relatively unproven; a variety of professional mathematicians and educators question the need for change.

Frank Allen, former president of the NCTM, Professor Emeritus of mathematics at Elmhurst College, and a high school mathematics teacher for 35 years, firmly believes that secondary school mathematics curriculum must be organized around its own internal structure, not around an artificial structure such as problem solving or real-world applications. Students should be introduced to the idea that mathematics is a hierarchy of propositions forged by logic on a postulational base in ninth grade and that concept should be thoroughly established in the student's mind by grade 12 (Allen, 1996, p. 1).

> "As Americans cheered the shuttle flight lift-off on July 23, 1999, with its extraordinary scientific payload, few knew how much mathematics and physics knowledge was involved to achieve this latest mastery of outer space. Few know that, in 1997, the latest year for which statistics are available, only 3,826 bachelor's degrees in physics were awarded, the lowest figure in 40 years. Fully half the students entering graduate classes in 1998 were foreign born."
> —DeWeese, August 2, 1999 [On-line]

Your decision about whether to integrate subject matter across a three- or four-year time block or to continue using the traditional subject-matter organizational structure in your high school will dictate choice of textbooks, teaching methodologies, and use of technology. The principal problem with the integrated format has nothing to do with integrating instruction per se; good teachers have always integrated, and good programs have always been somewhat integrated. Many of the TIMSS countries integrate their curricula (Japan Society of Mathematical Education, 1990, January, pp. 33–43). There are two major differences, however, between integrated curriculum as it is designed and used in Japan, for example, and the programs developed to align with the NCTM Standards. First, most laypersons (e.g., parents or taxpayers) are unable to evaluate an NCTM-based integrated program to determine if students will receive an adequate amount of coverage of algebra, geometry, trigonometry, and so on. In Japan, although the curriculum is integrated, the amount and difficulty of specific subjects like algebra I, geometry, and algebra II are mandated and monitored. Second, in the NCTM-based integrated programs, content definitely plays second fiddle to process; the treatment of important mathematical ideas is slighted to favor real-world applications and authentic problem-solving; and there is an overemphasis, and in some cases an alarming dependency, on calculator usage. Unfortunately, student assessment is far more difficult, both formatively and summatively, when using integrated mathematics programs because material is not taught for mastery per se.

The following practices hold the most promise for raising and maintaining high school mathematics achievement:

◆ Constant articulation with middle school and elementary school faculty to ensure that prerequisite mathematical knowledge is being taught in a way that permits students to be successful in high school after they have done well in elementary and middle school. Care must be taken in the structuring of such meetings to concentrate on problem solving and to avoid blame.

◆ A continued emphasis on both instruction and practice regarding facility in two-way translation between language and mathematical symbolism.

◆ Cultivation of the idea that mathematics is interesting for its own sake and need not constantly be rooted in real-world applications. The acquisition of skills and knowledge requires more abstract and fundamentally pure mathematical learning at many points along a student's mathematical journey, and it is essential that they be included in your curriculum.

◆ An emphasis on the unique and indispensable contributions of mathematics to the development of the student's ability to think and communicate in a logical manner.

◆ A strong emphasis on proof and mathematical justification. Deductive reasoning is essential for the mastery of higher-level mathematics, and formal mathematical proofs are deductive reasoning. Unfortunately, proof and mathematical justification are not common aspects of U.S. lessons. In the TIMSS videotape study, deductive reasoning was found in 62% of the Japanese lessons, 21% of the German lessons, and 0% of the U.S. lessons (Stigler & Hiebert, 1997, January, p. 16).

◆ Caution in the use of calculators. "Taking the time to develop skill in the use of these devices is justified only to the extent that they improve the students' understanding of mathematics. Thousands of people have learned to use these devices without formal instruction; very few have learned mathematics that way" (Allen, 1996, p. 3).

◆ Reasonable demands on students' memory with the exception of the basic facts that should be memorized and the basic skills from each unit that should be habitualized.

◆ All students should have the *opportunity* to take four years of high school mathematics, choosing from the following courses (or an integrated sequence that includes the core courses of algebra I and II, geometry, and trigonometry) in high school: algebra I, geometry, algebra II, probability and statistics, trigonometry, linear algebra, mathematical analysis, and advanced placement (AP) calculus AB and BC. Mathematicians who teach college calculus generally feel that the only calculus worth taking in high school is AP calculus. A general calculus course wastes a semester or a year, and students frequently absorb much serious misinformation from it, making college calculus more difficult than it should be (Raimi, personal conversation, December 1999). Students who are reluctant or feel unable to take AP calculus should take more analytic geometry, linear algebra, or statistics. There are some who would question whether all students *can* succeed in the traditional algebra, geometry, and trigonometry-intermediate algebra sequence. You will never know the answer to that question unless your teachers raise their expectations while simultaneously offering the extra time and increased tutorials that some students may need.

### The Big Ideas in High School Math

1. Offer all students, regardless of ability level or prerequisite learnings, the opportunity to take four years of high school math.

2. Offer tutorials, Saturday school, and peer assistance for students who need help.

3.  Provide for differences in learning rates by offering different levels and different opportunities. This does not mean offering six different levels of remedial math, but offering algebra taught a number of different ways (computer-assisted instruction, independent study, small group tutorial, or Kumon math).

4.  Carefully monitor the quality and rigor of each course in the high school mathematics sequence. A strong mastery of algebra I is essential for success in algebra II. One of the great stumbling blocks for calculus students is their inadequate mastery of trigonometry. The trigonometry course that is offered must go beyond the "solution of triangles," which was the rationale for trigonometry from the time of Ptolemy to about 1950. In addition, it must study the trigonometric functions as functions, analytically and graphically, including exercise in proving identities and solving trigonometric equations.

5.  Develop a plan to monitor the mathematics achievement of all students to assess curricular and instructional effectiveness. Be able to answer questions such as: How does the achievement of students who have teacher A compare with students who have teacher B? What percentage of at-risk students drops out of math on a yearly basis? What percentage of students take and receive a passing grade on the AP calculus examinations?

> "Next time you leave your home, get into your car, and drive down the road to the shopping centre, reflect on this: none of it would be there had we been unable to use numbers. Trade, architecture, road building, complex manufacturing, money—all depend on numbers. Numbers are the language of science, and yet thinking about the world in terms of numbers is as natural and as human as talking. To understand the world, and our place in it, we need to understand our innate gift for numbers."
> —Butterworth, 1999, p. 351

## Math Disabilities

### Why Do Some Students Fail to Learn Math and What Can We Do About It?

Despite the fact that all children come to school with intuitive skills about math, a substantial percentage of them do not become proficient in mathematics. Why do some students fail to achieve their potential? Why do others simply fail and give up? There are no easy answers to this question, but there are some hypotheses.

1.  Children do not read well and consequently cannot comprehend what they read in the mathematics textbook with any more understanding than they can comprehend what they read from other textbooks or library books (Muth, 1984). Even many good readers cannot read math well because they fail to understand that different reading skills and even a different reading speed are required. In reading mathematics, every word is important.

2.  Some important mathematical knowledge may have been taught and even partially learned, but for lack of practice and further instruction it has not been adequately retained.

3.  Some misconceptions derive from instruction that is inadvertently unclear to students. Explanations may have been inadequate, leaving students with misconceptions, or too few good examples were presented.

4. Poor basic arithmetic skills make problem solving particularly difficult. The inability to automatically retrieve basic facts from long-term memory makes the solving of word problems more demanding because students have to use more time-consuming counting strategies to complete the computational aspects of the word problem. Whether the problems with fact retrieval are because of memory deficits or lack of will to commit the facts to memory must be determined by further investigation. Some children need specialized training to improve their retrieval deficits. Although reading disabilities have been widely researched, research in the area of mathematical disabilities is relatively sparse (Sutaria, 1985). "The review of cognitive, neuropsychological, and genetic correlates of mathematical achievement and mathematical disorder, however, suggests that there exist real deficits that affect mathematical learning and performance" (Geary, 1994, p. 187).

## The Big Ideas in Dealing with Mathematical Disabilities

1. Stay tuned for the current research that is being done by the National Institute of Child Health and Human Development. It will be several years until all of the results are in, but much more should be known about the early learning of mathematics and how to prevent and remediate math disabilities.

2. Do not ignore the math-reading connection when considering the source of a math disability.

3. When in doubt, begin at the beginning—not with memorization of math facts or basic algorithms, but with a child's understanding of numeration. Before designing any remediation program, find out through testing interviews and observation what a child believes and understands about mathematics.

Raising mathematics achievement is a complicated task. To accomplish it, you are dependent on teachers for good instruction, textbook publishers for well-written textbooks, students for motivation and willingness to put forth the effort to learn, parents to support the school's and their children's efforts, and central office administrators to assist with curricular and budgetary issues. After that list, you may feel there is very little over which you have any control at all. You are a bit like the maestro of an orchestra, however. You are not responsible for playing each instrument; in fact, you don't even have to know how to play them. But you are the only one who can lift the baton and bring harmony from such a disparate group of individuals, each playing a different instrument and a different set of notes. Without the maestro, the orchestra is merely cacophony. Without instructional leadership your teachers, students, and parents are merely people who happen to be connected to the same school. Under your leadership all of the people can come together to make beautiful music—in this case, mathematics achievement. Without you, there may be spots of brilliance here and there, but the overall performance is almost certain to be panned by the reviewers.

Chapter 6 describes the importance of instructional leadership and shows how you can lead your school to improving mathematics achievement.

# The Practicalities of Raising Math Achievement

*"One of the most widely accepted ideas within the mathematics education community is the idea that students should understand mathematics. The goal of many research and implementation efforts in mathematics education has been to promote learning with understanding. But achieving this goal has been like searching for the Holy Grail. There is a persistent belief in the merits of the goal, but designing school learning environments that successfully promote understanding has been difficult."*

—Hiebert & Carpenter, 1992, p. 65

esigning school learning environments that "successfully promote understanding" is vastly different from buying new textbooks or hiring a consultant to do some staff development. Designing school learning environments requires an understanding of the culture and climate of your school as well as an intimate knowledge of its history of improvement and change.

We are all on the outlook for the magic bullet or the quick fix, something we can do and see instant results. We are as susceptible to what Venesky calls "snake oil and charismatic solutions" (Palmaffy, 1997 [On-line]) as dieters are to the newest quick weight loss schemes being touted on a cable television infomercial. Our quest for meaningful and sustained change, however, is an elusive one.

"For more than a hundred years much complaint has been made of the unmethodological way in which schools are conducted, but it is only within the last thirty that any serious attempt has been made to find a remedy for this state of things.

And with what results? Schools remain exactly as they were" (Comenius, 1632/1967, p. 295).

Often the innovation we adopt *is* merely snake oil, and we're delighted when it dies a natural death; we surreptitiously stash the manuals, thousands of dollars worth of expensive equipment, and dusty binders filled with consultants' handouts into the dumpster and thankfully move on to the next implementation. But sometimes worthy, research-based improvements that should become institutionalized because they get results, fail for the following simple reasons (Latham, 1988, pp. 42–43):

▶ Doing something brand new takes more work, and not everyone embraces working harder. Consultants are good at making complicated things seem simple during their dog and pony shows, but when the consultants fly home, the practitioners are left to make it happen.

▶ Educators forget (if they ever really understood) that the innovations they adopt to change the kids usually require that they change also. Principals and teachers may be required to give up long-standing past practices and learn different methodologies. Most educators don't rank high on the scale of risk takers and if the leap of faith is too large, they will remain quietly on the sidelines of disbelief.

▶ Change requires discipline. Learning to do something new requires attention to detail, practice of unfamiliar skills, and the desire for further training. These processes demand collaboration and teamwork while, typically, teachers enjoy autonomy, routine, and the freedom to do their own thing.

▶ "Rome wasn't built in a day." Our students are not the only ones with short attention spans. Educators want instant results, and when they are not forthcoming, they abandon their plans with scarcely a backward look.

▶ We doubt research and disbelieve evidence. We're often accused of paying more attention to fads and fashion, than science (Lally & Price, 1997 [On-line]). We're suspicious of data, statistics, and norm-referenced tests. Even when we get the results we want on standardized tests, we're loathe to believe that specific teaching methods, higher expectations, or the materials we used really made a difference. We attribute our results (as my own teachers did when standardized test scores began to rise) to chance or a "good group of kids." Of course, that's because if we're responsible for good news, then we will also be accountable for bad news, a troubling prospect for many educators.

▶ We doubt common sense and disbelieve our own experience. Fad and fashion often lure us into leaving behind common sense practices and methodologies that produced results, but we're led to believe that new is often better and that the traditional is outdated.

▶ Programs depend on people, and when key supporters and leaders leave, the energy and momentum that kept a program going may dissipate almost overnight. So if you think you might be moving on, don't ask your faculty to get behind a massive improvement plan. Your departure will only serve to make them more cynical than they already were about improvement.

▶ Constant and ongoing training is necessary to keep a program viable. Every time a new staff member comes aboard, a program will be watered down and become less effective unless that individual receives quality training. Educators are notorious for not following through on this commitment, so eventually there remain only a few old-timers who are still using a methodology or approach that when practiced by an entire staff was extraordinarily powerful.

▶ Lack of supervision and accountability are major stumbling blocks to successful change. Somebody has to care about these two critical issues, and the building principal is the go-to person for making sure and keeping track. If you are not organized, structured, and data-driven, find someone to help you who is (e.g., a lead teacher, a building secretary, or a school improvement coordinator).

This lengthy introduction, filled with reasons for the failure of innovations and improvement, may seem a morbid way to begin, but it's very realistic. Forewarned is forearmed. If you are not prepared to build safeguards into your improvement initiative to help avoid these pitfalls, you are like those who fail to heed history and are therefore doomed to repeat it.

Bringing about meaningful change (i.e., higher mathematics achievement) is dependent on several critical things:

1. Instructional leadership

2. Shared decision making

3. Careful planning

4. Parental support and involvement

5. A well-designed accountability system

6. A sufficient length of time

*Principals Do Make a Difference: Instructional Leadership*

What you do on a daily basis in your unique school setting makes a difference in how much and how well the students in your school learn. Your ability to respond to the organizational and environmental context in which you work and to communicate a powerful vision for your school directly influences your teachers' expectations for their students and the students' opportunity to learn. This in turn creates a positive effect on student achievement in mathematics. When teachers perceive their principals as strong instructional leaders, students achieve more (Andrews & Soder, 1987; Heck, Larson, & Marcoulides, 1990; Heck, Marcoulides, & Lang, 1991).

How can you determine if your teachers think you are a strong instructional leader? Ask them! If you want to raise mathematics achievement in your school, you must begin with a healthy dose of self-examination and a commitment to the following seven steps (McEwan, 1998b, p. 13):

1. Establish clear instructional goals.

2. Be there for your staff.

3. Create a school culture and climate conducive to learning.

4. Communicate the vision and mission of your school.

5. Set high expectations for your staff.

6. Develop teacher leaders.

7. Maintain positive attitudes toward students, staff, and parents.

> *"A group of people is not a team. A team is a group of people with a high degree of interdependence geared toward the achievement of a goal or completion of a task. In other words, they agree on a goal and agree that the only way to achieve the goal is to work together."*
> —Parker, 1990, p. 16

*You Can't Do It All on Your Own: Shared Decision Making*

Lest you feel totally burdened with the overwhelming responsibility of single-handedly raising mathematics achievement in your school, be assured that you don't have to do it alone. My training for the principalship included some passing references to participatory management and group decision making, but my job description led me to believe that I was personally responsible for doing it all. Fortunately I was rescued from that mindset when the concept of Building Leadership teams was introduced to our district. After the training period, our team met one full afternoon per month charting a course for school improvement and tackling the substantive issues related to teaching and learning. My staff members were definitely more committed to implementation when they were involved from the very beginning in making important decisions about how to reach our goals. Shared decision making has also been shown to increase job satisfaction (Ashton & Webb, 1986, pp. 95–97), create ownership leading to a more positive attitude toward the organization (Beers, 1984), and create a more professional environment within the school (Apelman, 1986, pp. 115–129). After your team is formed, get training to help the group become cohesive and productive. You cannot expect a team to develop a collaborative working relationship instantaneously. If necessary, use a consultant or other resources to help your team develop the skills and trust it needs to be successful (McEwan, 1997).

Now that you're on your way to becoming an outstanding instructional leader and have put together a team of knowledgeable and dedicated teachers who recognize a need for change, your next step is to develop a plan.

*Look Before You Leap: Planning for Change*

Planning for change involves setting goals, but goals that are too numerous or too vague will frustrate teachers. A good goal statement must include the following five elements (Policy Studies Associates, 1998, p. 54):

1. The baseline: the level at which students are currently performing (e.g., 15% of the student body is sufficiently prepared to take algebra I in eighth grade as measured by receiving a passing grade on the Orleans-Hanna Algebra Prognosis Test, Third Edition [Hanna, 1999], but some of the students who are eligible and who do enroll are dropping out of the course before it ends)

2. The goal: what you want to happen (e.g., increase by 15% the number of students who are eligible to take algebra I in the eighth grade and who also succeed at it)

3. The outcome indicator: the measure that will be used to demonstrate success (e.g., students will be evaluated for their readiness to take and master algebra I with the Orleans-Hanna; students will be determined to have mastered the class when they can pass the state algebra I exam, the Regents exam, or some other agreed-upon measure of algebra I achievement)

4. The standard or performance level: the level of success that shows substantial progress (e.g., a passing score on the algebra I achievement test)

5. The time frame: the timeline for accomplishing the goals, indicating how much progress you hope to achieve after one year, two years and three years (e.g., a 5% increase in the number of students by the end of year one, a 10% increase by the end of year two, and a 15% increase by the end of year three)

> "Problems are our friends because only through immersing ourselves in problems can we come up with creative solutions. Problems are the route to deeper change and deeper satisfaction. In this sense, effective organizations embrace problems rather than avoid them."
> —Fullan & Miles, 1992, p. 750

There are many excellent and inexpensive resources to guide your schoolwide improvement efforts (Educational Testing Service, 1996; RMC Research Corporation, 1995; WestEd, 1997). Which one you use is less important than that you choose a framework and stick to it.

The National Center to Improve the Tools of Educators (NCITE) has developed a handbook (1997 [On-line]) that will lead you and your team through four important stages:

1. Setting improvement goals

2. Defining the scope of the improvement plan

3. Selecting tools and practices for the improvement plan

4. Planning and implementing

Let's follow a math task force as they consider how to raise mathematics achievement in their school using this model.

### Step 1: Setting Improvement Goals in Mathematics Education

Determine what your students are not doing compared to what they should be doing as measured by a test of your choosing. A small group of faculty at the Meadow Brook School (not an actual school) approached their principal, Sarah Abels, about changing to a new mathematics curriculum based on the NCTM Standards. They had recently been to a conference and heard a speaker who excited them about the possibilities. When the math task force examined the test scores they found that overall their students actually performed quite well on the standardized test given yearly by the district. When the data was disaggregated, however, the lower 20% of the students scored far lower than most teachers were aware. This uncovered a serious problem that needed to be addressed immediately. A small group of teachers felt that the standardized test contained too few problem-solving opportunities and over-emphasized computation, so there was no real way of knowing how well their students could solve difficult word problems. So Sarah and her teachers administered the Stanford Diagnostic Mathematics Test, Fourth Edition (Harcourt Inc., 1999), which emphasizes problem solving and problem-solving strategies to ascertain the accuracy of the teachers' perceptions. The tests were administered to every student in Grades 3 through 6. The results validated the teachers' perceptions, and a need for improvement in the problem-solving abilities of all students was clearly established. The task force formulated a two-part goal: raising the overall mathematics achievement of a specific group of targeted students who were achieving well below grade level in all areas of math and increasing the problem-solving abilities of all students in Grades 3 through 6. The meeting was adjourned and the group agreed that during the next meeting they would get down to defining the details of their improvement plan.

## Step 2: Defining the Scope of the Improvement Plan

At the next meeting the task force realized that they needed more information before they could determine the scope of the improvement plan. Although increasing their students' problem-solving abilities was the goal, they had no idea why their students had low problem-solving abilities. It seemed that teachers were doing an excellent job of teaching computation skills and that students definitely had the tools they needed to solve problems. Why were students unable to use these tools successfully? Someone suggested looking at the students who had low reading comprehension scores to see how many of them had also received low scores in problem solving. Someone else volunteered to examine the student texts currently in use at each grade level to see how many high-quality and difficult problems were actually included for teachers to use and what kind and how many examples were provided for helping students to gain problem-solving strategies. A third member of the task force volunteered to survey the staff to determine how frequently word problems were the focus of instruction and how comfortable teachers felt discussing difficult problems with their students. Another task force member agreed to investigate translation problems experienced by middle-grade students and to develop a list of recommendations for teachers based on the research.

## Step 3: Selecting Tools and Practices for the Improvement Plan

The eager teachers meanwhile continued to press for purchasing the problem-solving curriculum immediately. It was highly recommended by a third-grade team in a neighboring school district who had been using it for one year. Sarah insisted on requesting a packet of research from the company. Unfortunately the research was disappointing both in quantity and quality. "Research should be of high quality and ample enough to justify widespread adoption of an approach and the accompanying expenditure of funds and effort" (NCITE [On-line]). Since Meadow Brook School was considering implementing this innovative curriculum in all of its grades and classrooms, which involved more than 800 students, Sarah carefully considered the following NCITE recommendations. "If a large-scale improvement is required, then the school must select approaches that (a) have proven successful in other wide-scale improvement efforts, or (b) have proven successful in a medium-scale implementation and include a plan for expansion that indicates there is a strong likelihood that the approach will be uniformly successful in a large-scale effort" (NCITE [On-line]). The task force wisely decided that a large-scale implementation using materials for which they did not have an adequate research base would be inadvisable, although they did not totally dismiss the idea of using the recommended materials for a small-scale trial in several classrooms if it included a well-structured assessment component. Of special concern to the teachers were the diverse learners at each grade level (e.g., special education students, at-risk students, and students with limited English proficiency). Since these students were not achieving at the desired levels overall, special attention had to be paid to their needs. Students with potentially higher failure rates must always be carefully monitored during any kind of experimentation.

## Step 4: Planning and Implementing the Improvement Plan

The investigation of reading levels uncovered a correlation between poor problem-solving abilities and low reading comprehension. Teachers began to talk in depth about how they could integrate the teaching of comprehension strategies with their mathematics lessons, a new idea for most. The subcommittee that had been asked to investigate possible curricula for the lowest-achieving mathematics students presented the research they had found on *Connecting Math Concepts* (SRA/McGraw-Hill, 1991) and its success with diverse learners. The results were impressive and the committee noted that the experimental groups in the studies were very similar in demographics to the students of their school (Direct Instruction Consumer Reports, 1996 [On-line]).

The parents of the students who were selected to participate in the limited pilot of the problem-solving curriculum were notified in the spring prior to the implementation year. A meeting was held to answer questions regarding the implementation, and parents who objected to the implementation had the option of placing their child with a teacher who would be using the established math program.

Not only were plans laid for a summative, standardized assessment to be given during late spring of the implementation year, but also several formative assessments were planned at critical points throughout the school year. The district's assessment specialist helped the team design a plan to measure students' gain scores in mathematics during the implementation year to be compared to their gain scores during earlier years. In this way the team could consider each individual child's progress as well as the group's average achievement. The gain score method would be especially helpful for evaluating the impact of the pilot implementation on diverse learners.

After examining the textbooks currently in use, the task force found ample examples and opportunities for problem solving, but determined that teachers lacked confidence in their own abilities in this area. The task force recommended staff development in this area and asked a local graduate student who had spent a year with a Japanese research-lesson group to share his experiences and talk about the characteristics of excellent problem-solving instruction. They invited him to observe in classrooms and to conference with individual teachers and the principal.

After one year of implementation, the mathematics task force met to review the test results. The gain scores for diverse learners were smaller using the problem-solving curriculum than they had been in the previous year; several diverse learners actually made no gains. Although several gifted students had enormous gain scores using the problem-solving curriculum, sufficient to boost the overall grade level score substantially, there were no significant differences in the gain scores of the majority of individual students, particularly those scoring in the third quartile (between the 50th and 75th percentiles) on the standardized test. Although problem-solving ability continued to be a major goal for the Meadow Brook faculty, their year-long implementation demonstrated that the curriculum they had originally chosen was not the total answer to their problem. The program was definitely worthy of consideration for gifted students, but it did not produce the desired results with at-risk learners. The task force discussed the possibility that diverse teacher expectations were also a variable that might have had an adverse impact on the gain scores. They examined the gain scores of gifted students compared to at-risk students in the three classrooms to see if they could detect any subtle patterns that might reveal such trends. And they considered the possibility that the lack of improvement in certain groups of students was due to an inadequate mathematical foundation and that teachers may have incorrectly assumed mastery of prior material.

As you work with your mathematics task force or school improvement team to plan for change, consider the process from several perspectives.

First, provide plenty of research and resource materials, speakers, and site visits so that team members can make decisions from a sound knowledge base. Don't reinvent the wheel, but don't rush out to duplicate what someone else has done either. Consider your student body, your faculty, and your parent community before you make a change. For example, if you decide that new textbooks need to be chosen, leave no stone unturned in gathering resource materials and research studies. Don't rush to judgment.

Next, encourage every faculty member to be brutally honest about which of the alterable variables they believe are creating the most serious roadblocks to achievement (e.g., low expectations, lack of a common set of values regarding grades and homework, and inconsistent instruction across a grade level). Structure a group process in which every member of the group is expected to contribute ideas. If teachers are reluctant to speak in front of others, use a questionnaire or small focus groups to gather information that can then be shared in the large group by a spokesperson. "It is no simple matter to reform teaching, learning, and the supporting conditions that fuel and refuel the moral purpose of teaching" (Fullan, 1994, p. 79).

Last, make sure that enough time is given for all points of view to be heard and understood. Shutting down discussion and dissent will result in a fragmented implementation.

*Get Mom and Dad on Your Side: The Importance of Parental Involvement*

Parental involvement and support are crucial to raising mathematics achievement in your school. One way in which we garnered parental support and involvement was through publishing what we called our "I Can Learn" booklet. This booklet set forth the outcomes in reading, writing, and mathematics for all grade levels so parents knew what we expected their children to learn. We also included a set of teacher expectations (e.g., the teacher is expected to provide quality instruction for all students, to hold students accountable for following school rules and completing assignments, and to evaluate and communicate student progress to parents and students) as well as expectations for parents and students. This document sent the message to parents that we were serious about learning and that we must all be accountable (teachers, parents, and students) if we were to reach our goals.

I believe that when parents observe the following evidence in your school they will back you 100%:

> "When a process makes people feel that they have a voice in matters that affect them, they will have a greater commitment to the overall enterprise and will take greater responsibility for what happens to the enterprise. The absence of such a process insures that no one feels responsible, that blame will always be directed externally, that adversarialism will be a notable feature of school life."
> —Sarason, 1990, p. 61

► Evidence of children (theirs and others') learning through both formative and published summative evaluations

► Evidence of teaching effectiveness as observed by parents when they are participating in the life of the school as a volunteer or visitor (e.g., frequent planned events that bring parents into classrooms to observe)

► Evidence of educators' desires to make parents a part of the learning team through advisory groups, through inclusion on the building leadership team, and through periodic surveys that ask for parental input

There are six important things that parents can do to assist in your achievement initiative:

1. Discuss their children's mathematics homework with them. In order to do this, it is imperative that parents understand your curriculum and support it. Parents have every right to insist that mathematics textbooks come home. When students don't have textbooks, particularly in grades 5 and up, they *and* their parents get lost. It is surprising how much a student can learn when they have a book, a parent, and the correct answers toward which they are working in the solution of a problem.

2. Visit their children's mathematics teacher to find out how their children are learning and how they can help. This requires that teachers have an open-door policy and are able to explain what they are doing in lay language. Educational and mathematical jargon are not acceptable means of communication.

3. Insist that in the eighth grade their children enroll in algebra I (or in a similarly demanding course that includes algebraic concepts) and in more advanced math and science courses in high school so they can keep all of their future options open.

4. Ensure that their children are gaining the groundwork for success in algebra through a rigorous curriculum in kindergarten and in grades 1 through 7 that moves beyond arithmetic and prepares them for the transition to algebra.

5. Help their children understand the importance of taking challenging mathematics and science courses to their future by visiting colleges, familiarizing them with college requirements, and exploring financial aid options available to students.

6. Show the importance of mathematics for career choices by talking with their children about the use of mathematics in their work or the work of adults they know (U.S. Department of Education, 1997 [On-line]).

When parents are unable for whatever reason to do some or all of these things, offer assistance through the guidance or counseling offices. Raising expectations for students and giving them opportunities to expand their horizons is a critical responsibility of both mathematics teachers and guidance counselors.

*What Gets Measured Gets Done: Assessment and Accountability*

If you want to lead your school toward excellence in mathematics achievement, you must become an evaluation-minded principal (Nevo, 1991). You must constantly evaluate the teaching effectiveness of your staff, the mathematics proficiency of your students, and the overall effectiveness of your programs. Evaluation in each of these areas must be both summative and formative (Scriven, 1967). "Summative evaluation offers a final determination of the worth of a program or individual's performance in a role. It is not designed to be constructive; rather it is designed to be ultimately judgmental and primarily used by those stakeholders who will make some decision about program or individual continuation. Formative evaluation, on the other hand, is conceptualized as constructive. In both roles, evaluation serves to inform decision making" (Goldring & Rallis, 1993, pp. 96–97).

How will you and your team determine your student body's level of numeracy? That decision should be made before you launch into your mathematics improvement plan. If you're going to use a different measure of student achievement than you have presently been using, administer a pretest to all of the students in order to gather baseline data. If testing is to be meaningful and helpful to classroom teachers it must track the performance and progress of each student in your school over several years. The tests should be standardized and administered yearly to every student. I am aware of the popularity of performance assessments and believe they are an ideal way for teachers to assess students in the classroom, but my experiences in constructing and administering performance tests at the district level in math and science has led me to agree wholeheartedly with these authors:

"On the basis of the data examined, we are forced to conclude that constructed response items provide less information in more time at greater cost than do multiple choice items. This conclusion is surely discouraging to those who feel that constructed response items are more authentic and hence, in some sense, more useful than multiple-choice items" (Lukhele, Thissen, & Wainer, 1994, p. 245).

I am also aware of the controversy over testing students who have limited English proficiency and learning disabilities. Many states are excluding larger numbers of students each year, and, not surprisingly, achievement scores rise. This is not the kind of improvement you should be looking for. Although my state and district offered testing exemptions to these populations, as a principal I wanted to know how effective our efforts were at helping diverse learners join the mainstream. To know that an individual student has made substantial gains in achievement (even if he or she is still below grade level) is far more instructive than knowing the composite reading score of a particular grade level or of the school as a whole. We examined the longitudinal test scores of each of our students to determine their progress over time. We tracked the type of teachers with whom they experienced the most success. We expected our target students (those who were well below grade level) to overcome huge deficits in performance through our interventions, and seeing those results in black and white was highly motivating to teachers. Gains in mathematics achievement are made one student at a time. We also disaggregated our data to determine how well we were serving the students in various subpopulations. Overall

"We strongly recommend that school districts [schools] clearly define their understanding of the desired end result early in the change process."
—Harrison, Killion, & Mitchell, 1989, p. 56

> "The purpose of evaluation includes, but goes beyond, accountability. Evaluation looks at programs and personnel and seeks to discover why the programs have had the determined effect and whether the determined effect is one that the school community wants."
> —Goldring & Rallis, 1993, p. 92

improvement in mathematics achievement that is based only on the achievement of students in the top quartile means that you are achieving quality without equity, a condition that discriminates against your students in the bottom quartile.

When you're planning how to summatively evaluate the success of your implementation, don't overlook the importance of formative evaluation, the ongoing monitoring of a program that will help you determine if any students or teachers are falling through the cracks. The purpose of formative testing is to provide information to the learner and to the teacher about what the learner knows.

Do not hesitate to ask for help with assessment and accountability. Possible sources for technical assistance include

▶ A test company consultant who will work with your staff to understand the construction of standardized tests and how they can be utilized to evaluate your program

▶ A university professor who can be hired to provide the evaluation component of your plan

▶ Central office staff who have expertise in this area

▶ A consultant from the state department of education

Assessment is essential to improvement. Without continuous monitoring of progress you will be unable to answer questions about specific individuals or groups of students. "It is the action around assessment—the discussions, meetings, revisions, arguments, and opportunities to continually create new directions for teaching, learning, curriculum, and assessment—that ultimately have consequence. The 'things' of assessment are essentially useful as dynamic supports for reflection and action, rather than as static products with value in and of themselves" (Darling-Hammond, Ancess, & Falk, 1995, p. 18).

## Take Your Time: The Five-Year Plan

Implementing an improvement initiative takes time and if you fast forward through any of the critical stages, you will fail. As important as vision is, beware of becoming blinded by your own. "The principal who is committed to a particular innovation or philosophy may pursue it in such narrow and self-defeating ways that key teachers will resist the idea until the principal leaves or is transferred. In other cases the principal is 'apparently successful' in getting teachers to use the innovation while failing to achieve more basic changes in enabling them to consider alternatives, reflect on their practices, and otherwise improve" (Fullan, 1992, p. 19). Take the time needed for goal setting, planning, training, implementation, fine-tuning, and evaluation. Consider alternatives and listen to teachers who may have questions or concerns. Teachers typically go through a variety of stages on their way to successfully implementing a new program; don't push them faster than they can go. Begin small if necessary. "The objective of evolutionary planning is to capitalize on the 'low risk' quality of smaller-scale innovation to increase certainty. This, in turn, increases motivation and the possibility of concerted, more 'tightly coupled' action across the school" (Louis & Miles, 1990, p. 211). Be sensitive to how much change your teachers can handle at one time and be prepared to celebrate small successes and gradual improvements.

Raising mathematics achievement in your school will require the concerted effort of many individuals—administrators, teachers, parents, and, most especially, students. Do not forget that it is the students who actually sharpen their No. 2 pencils and sit down to take the tests that will measure your success. Good breakfasts and pep assemblies with cheerleaders can never take the place of solid instruction and hard work every single day of the school year—year after year after year. Achievement, not activity, is your goal. Dogged determination is preferred to bursts of brilliance. Raising mathematics achievement is often messy; improvement is never neat and circumscribed. There will be arguments, discussions, conflict, and territorialism. You must be the facilitator. There will be uncertainties and questions. You must grow accustomed to ambiguity and learn to live with approximation. There will be weariness and discouragement. You must help staff members appreciate small steps forward even though you are looking for more dramatic improvements. Be prepared for teachers and parents who want to move too quickly and for a like number of folks who do not want to move at all. Remember the analogy from Chapter 5. You are the maestro. You alone have the power to create a symphony from cacophony. Accept the challenge and pick up the baton.

*"Time is the most valuable thing a man [or a school] can spend."*
—*Theophrastus, 278 B.C.*

# Thirty-Plus Things
# You Can Do in Your School
# to Raise Math Achievement

*H*ere are more than 30 programs, suggestions, and ideas to investigate, implement, and integrate; each one has the potential to boost mathematics achievement. You will find activities and programs to motivate students to increase their mathematical knowledge, ways to help teachers become more effective, and things you can do as an instructional leader to communicate your vision of a mathematically excellent school.

## *MATHCOUNTS*

MATHCOUNTS is a national math coaching and competition program that promotes seventh- and eighth-grade mathematics. The goal is to make math achievement as challenging, exciting and prestigious as a school sport. Teachers and volunteers use specially prepared materials to coach student "mathletes," either as part of in-class instruction or as an extracurricular activity. Students compete in more than 500 local meetings held in February around the country, winners progress to state contests in March, and finally, there is a national competition in May. Encourage your faculty and parents to become MATHCOUNTS coaches and sponsors. This activity is guaranteed to raise achievement for every student who participates. Carol Gambill's students (see the Gambill Method in Chapter 5) took first place in the Pittsburgh MATHCOUNTS Competition for five consecutive years and were the Pennsylvania State MATHCOUNTS Champions two years ago. She highly recommends this activity to build superior problem solving skills. Don't just limit participation to gifted students. Get as many of your students as you can involved. For more information, check out the Web site at *http://mathcounts.org.*

## A First-Grade Math Lesson

*A First-Grade Lesson with David Burchfield* is a videotape produced by the North Central Regional Educational Laboratory that tracks a teacher throughout the school day as he attempts to strike a balance between teacher- and student-directed learning. The 50-minute videotape is accompanied by a guidebook and makes an excellent starting point for discussions regarding what an ideal math lesson should include. To order, contact the North Central Regional Educational Laboratory, (800) 356-2745. Order item # SDL-DB-95.

## Ask Dr. Math

Introduce your teachers to Ask Dr. Math and Teacher2Teacher, two services of the Math Forum, an on-line community for math educators and parents. Teachers are invited to submit questions about mathematics instruction or to search the archives for past questions and answers. Everything you ever wanted to ask or know about math instruction can be found here. The doctor is in 24 hours a day at *http://forum.swarthmore.edu/dr.math.*

## SuperMath

SuperMath is a unique computer-based problem-solving approach to prealgebra concepts for Grades 4 through 10. This program makes an ideal supplement to a direct instruction math program and can also serve as an after-school math program for Title I and Gifted students. In one of the most intriguing units, "Word Problem Processors," students figure out how to solve word problems by communicating with a space creature stuck inside the computer that understands English and speaks math. The program enables students to construct their own sense of how language and math interact. Other units have such catchy and highly motivating titles as "Golf Challenge," "Carchitect," "Mega MacBurger World," and "Where in the Hood Is Carmen Sandecimal?" For more information, call (800) 999-0153.

## Accelerated Math

Accelerated Math is an algorithm-based computer program that covers traditional math topics of third through seventh grades as well as prealgebra, algebra 1 and 2, geometry, precalculus, and calculus. It can be housed and managed in the school library, a mathematics laboratory, or an individual classroom and is available for both the Macintosh and PC. While the program should certainly not take the place of classroom instruction, it provides a way to motivate students who need additional practice or more personalized assignments than the classroom teacher is able to provide. There are additional sets of questions that include integrative, authentic, performance-based assignments and projects that are scored by teachers with provided scoring rubrics. Visit the Web site at *http://www.advlearn.com* for further information.

## Kumon Math

Kumon Math has traditionally been taught at learning centers in which parents enroll their children on a fee basis for mathematics remediation or enrichment. Public and private schools have recently adopted the methodology. Kumon Math was developed by a Japanese mathematician, Toru Kumon, to help his son learn elementary math. Today there are more than 2 million students enrolled in Kumon Centers around the world. The curriculum contains a set of carefully sequenced work sheets containing math problems. To move to a new level students must attain a required level of competence on a set of problems within a prescribed time span. The Kumon teachers call this the Standard Completion Time. There are some 3,800 work sheets, and students can move from the simplest of arithmetic to differential and integral calculus. Only when students have mastered a topic to fluency can they move on. Kumon (1991) says of his method: "Tedious and monotonous and repetitive this method might seem. But this in fact is a key to our method. So often elementary math amounts to a repulsive mystery to many children mainly because their teachers would think nothing of leaping all at once from the first or second stage to the task of adding five to a random selection of figures. This kind of jump must never be forced on children for it could be at once bewildering and baffling to some of them. Ours is an almost completely painless formula all the way" (p. 5). The key components of Kumon Math are independent learning, repeated practice, and mastery. Visit the Kumon Math Web site at *http://kumon.com* or call (800) ABC-MATH (222-6284) for more information. And if you have a Kumon Center in your community, stop by for a visit or ask to have some literature sent to you.

## Eisenhower Math Centers

The Eisenhower National Clearinghouse for Math and Science (on-line) provides resources to assist you with math instruction. Its home page describes exemplary materials, teaching methods, and assessment resources for kindergarten through Grade 12. The Clearinghouse collaborates with existing regional and national networks and coordinates its activities and resources with the Eisenhower Regional Consortia for Mathematics and Science. You can find the Clearinghouse at *http://www.enc.org/*. Access the resources of your region at the following Web sites: Appalachia Region *http://www.ael.org* (Kentucky, Tennessee, Virginia, and West Virginia); Mid-Continent Region *http://www.mcrel.org* (Colorado, Kansas, Missouri, Nebraska, North Dakota, South Dakota, and Wyoming); Mid-Atlantic Region *http://www.rbs.org/eisenhower/index.html* (Delaware, Maryland, New Jersey, Pennsylvania, and Washington, D.C.); North Central Region *http://www.ncrel.org* (Illinois, Indiana, Iowa, Michigan, Minnesota, Ohio, and Wisconsin); Northeast and Island Region *http://www.terc.edu* (Connecticut, Maine, Massachusetts, New Hampshire, New York, Puerto Rico, Rhode Island, Vermont, and the Virgin Islands); Northwest Region *http://*

*www.col-ed.org* (Alaska, Idaho, Montana, Oregon, and Washington), Pacific Region *http://prel.hawaii.edu* (American Samoa, the Commonwealth of the Northern Mariana Islands, the Federated States of Micronesia, Guam, Hawaii, the Republic of the Marshall Islands, and the Republic of Palau); Southeastern Region *http://www.serve.org/Eisenhower* (Alabama, Florida, Georgia, Mississippi, North Carolina, and South Carolina); Southwestern Region *http://www.sedl.org* (Arkansas, Louisiana, New Mexico, Oklahoma, and Texas); Far West Region *http://www.enc.org* (Arizona, California, Nevada, and Utah).

## Rightstart

Rightstart is a program designed to provide the conceptual prerequisites for success in mathematics to students at risk for school failure (Griffin, Case, & Siegler, 1994). The program was tested in an experimental study over a period of three years with kindergarten students attending schools in Canada, California, and Massachusetts. The lessons taught to students in the experimental groups were based on a series of 30 interactive games that provided hands-on opportunities for children to develop numerical understandings. Students in the experimental groups achieved gains superior to the gains made by students in the control groups at the .05 level of significance. These gains were not only sustained into first grade but the students in the experimental group also had higher achievement on first-grade measures than students in the control groups. For more information about the Number Knowledge test and the Rightstart program, which is now called Number Worlds, contact Dr. Sharon Griffin at sgriffin@clarku.edu.

## Read About Math

Your students should find more to read than just fiction in your school's library. Encourage your librarian to purchase a wide selection of books about mathematics. There are many ways to showcase reading about math: Hold a Mathematics Book Fair; make math the theme of your next Reading Is Fundamental book giveaway; ask the librarian to feature math books during her read-alouds; encourage teachers (especially math teachers) to give "book talks" that feature math titles. Use *The Wonderful World of Mathematics: A Critically Annotated List of Children's Books in Mathematics* (Thiessen & Matthias, 1992) as a selection tool for elementary school libraries. Consult *The Magic of Mathematics: Discovering the Spell of Mathematics* (Pappas, 1994, pp. 315–320) and *200% of Nothing* (Dewdney, 1993, pp. 174–180) for dozens of titles that are suitable for middle and high school libraries.

## Equity 2000

In 1990 the College Board launched an initiative to increase minority enrollment in college preparatory mathematics courses. The program provides ongoing professional development to help teachers work with mixed-ability classes; trains administrators and teachers to use student enrollment and achievement data to drive school-based decision making; helps schools establish support services for students who need extra time to learn challenging content; and encourages and supports parents to become advocates on behalf of their children. Call (202) 822-5900 or visit the Web site at *http://www.collegeboard.org/equity/html/indx001.html*.

### Self-Assessment Guide for Improving Mathematics

This is an on-line instrument that contains questions relative to your school's progress in four areas:

1. Promoting equity and excellence

2. Promoting high-quality curricula and instruction

3. Promoting high-quality teachers

4. Coupling flexibility with responsibility for student performance

Print out this instrument to use with your improvement team by visiting the Web site at *http://www.ed.gov/inits/Math/chcklst.html*.

### E-Math

If you live in a community where mathematicians and engineers are in short supply, connect your students to mentors via e-mail. E-Math is an e-mail-based volunteer program designed to help students master challenging mathematics, science, and technology. There are several on-line options from which to choose; each one serves a different population of students. For example, the Electronic Mentoring Project uses telecommunications to enable Native American children living in remote rural areas to have access to information and resources. Visit their Web site at *http://www.tapr/4dinfosme.html*. Other E-Math programs are described at *http://www.ed.gov/pubs/emath/part1.html*.

### Math on the Web

Head to *http://www.webmath.com* and you'll find fascinating problem-solving advice for both students and teachers. Visitors to the site can just click on the type of problem they're solving (e.g., fractions, quadratic equations, personal finances, and geometry) and they'll be given blanks to fill in with the details of their problem.

### Japanese Math Challenge

This Web site, *http://www.japanese-online.com/math/index.htm*, provides an opportunity to check out math problems translated from Japan's junior high school math placement test, which is given to 12-year-olds. The 225 problems are logic based and consist of about 20 different types of story problems. This commercial site is designed to provide American students with quality math content based on world standards. After you've sampled the problems on the site, you may want to consider purchasing more problems from this commercial site, which is sponsored by Pacific Software Publishing.

## Achieve

Achieve is an independent, bipartisan, nonprofit organization overseen by the governors of 10 states (Illinois, Indiana, Maryland, Massachusetts, Michigan, New Hampshire, North Carolina, Vermont, Washington, and Wisconsin) and several corporate leaders. They are working together to develop strategies for raising mathematics achievement. Their goal is to develop a rigorous eighth-grade test, then identify instructional materials and professional development to help students and teachers prepare for it. To investigate how you might utilize the resources of Achieve, log on to *http://www.achieve.org/* or call (888) 200-0520.

## Project SEED

William Johntz, a remedial math teacher at Berkeley High School, founded Project SEED in 1963. He developed an approach that presents a curriculum of advanced mathematics for elementary students using a highly interactive teaching style, based on the Socratic questioning method. The program is used in school districts around the country, including in Dallas, Detroit, Indianapolis, the Philadelphia area, and the San Francisco Bay area (Ebrahami, May 26, 1999). Project SEED focuses primarily on at-risk and underserved populations and is especially interested in working with schools that focus on student academic success and place a high priority on improving achievement in mathematics. Visit Project Seed's Web site at *http://www.cofc.edu/ 7Ewayne/ps.home.html or call (510) 644-3422.*

## Extra Butter, Please

Crank up the VCR and show the TIMSS videotape: *Eighth-Grade Mathematics Lessons: United States, Japan, and Germany* (1997, September). A moderator's guide is available to help you lead the discussion. Even primary teachers will gain new insights about mathematics instruction from this unique and informative resource. You can purchase the complete set of materials, *Attaining Excellence: A TIMSS Resource Kit* (1997, September) by contacting the Superintendent of Documents, P.O. Box 371954, Pittsburgh, PA 15250-7954; telephone (202) 512-1800; fax: (202) 512-2250. The complete set includes the videotape, a moderator's guide to the tape, a summary of the TIMSS's findings, discussion guides for sharing the TIMSS information with various audiences (e.g., teachers and other community members), and a set of overheads to be used with presentations. Be sure to serve plenty of buttered popcorn.

## Helping Your Child Learn Math

This is the title of a free booklet for parents available from the U.S. Department of Education. The booklet contains activities related to geometry, algebra, measurement, statistics, and probability. You can request one free copy by calling (877) 433-7827, or download a PDF (portable document file) from *http://www.ed.gov/pubs/ parents/Math/*.

## What Can We Learn From the Japanese?

The answers to all of our math achievement problems cannot be found across the ocean. We do have a lot of the answers right here at home if we choose to pay attention to them. But, there is much that can be learned from studying how teachers in other countries and cultures approach math instruction. Gather a library of resource materials regarding this topic and form a study group. Emphasize to your teachers that the purpose of the group is to explore and learn, both from the materials you will read and from each other. Here's a brief list of resources to inform your discussions.

"A Lesson Is Like a Swiftly Flowing River: How Research Lessons Improve Japanese Education," an article by Lewis and Tsuchida in the *American Educator* (1998)

"The Japanese Model of Professional Development: Teaching As a Craft," an article by Shimahara in *Teaching and Teacher Education* (1998)

*Learning to Teach in Two Cultures: Japan and the United States* by Shimahara and Sakai (1995)

*The Teaching Gap* by Stigler and Hiebert (1999)

"Understanding and Improving Classroom Mathematics Instruction: An Overview of the TIMSS Video Study," an article by Stigler and Hiebert in the *Phi Delta Kappan* (1997)

## Lights, Camera, Action

Encourage your staff members to videotape one of their own math lessons. Suggest that they view the tape by themselves, not only to see what they do especially well, but also to determine what they might do to improve their mathematics instruction. Once they have viewed the tape, they are under no obligation to share it with anyone else, but encourage them to talk about the experience with a small discussion group or a colleague. Ask them to highlight one teaching behavior they intend to continue because it was so effective and one behavior they plan to eradicate as quickly as they can.

## MathStories.com

The goal of this Web site is to help elementary school students improve their math problem-solving skills. It includes math problems based on favorite children's books. Head to *http://www.mathstories.com*.

## Build a Professional Mathematics Library

Establish a small professional library of books about mathematics. Encourage teachers to personally read a book about mathematics during Sustained Silent Reading periods in their classroom and give a "book talk" during a faculty meeting. Here is a list to help you get started.

*Math: Facing an American Phobia* by Marilyn Burns (1998) — Marilyn Burns has written widely for parents and educators. This book is a quick read and a good introduction to the battle we're fighting.

*The Number Sense* by Stanislas Dehaene (1997) — Dehaene is a mathematician turned cognitive neuropsychologist, and his book will introduce you to the innate abilities for arithmetic that we all have.

*Children's Mathematical Development: Research and Practical Applications* by David Geary (1994) — If you only read one book about how children learn mathematics, read this one. It is well written, exceptionally well documented, and very solid.

*Children and Number: Difficulties in Learning Mathematics* by Martin Hughes (1986) — Hughes leads the reader through the important questions (and possible answers) regarding why some students have such a difficult time with mathematics.

*Knowing and Teaching Elementary Mathematics: Teachers' Understanding of Fundamental Mathematics in China and the United States* by Liping Ma (1999) — This is a fascinating study of how Chinese and American teachers approach the teaching of common mathematics topics in the elementary school. You'll wish you could go back and do it over again—the right way—after you read this book!

*Escalante: The Best Teacher in America* by Jay Mathews (1988) — Reporter Jay Mathews tells the compelling story of Jaime Escalante, a math teacher in East Los Angeles who helped his students overcome the odds and conquer AP calculus.

*Innumeracy: Mathematical Illiteracy and Its Consequences* by J. A Paulos (1988) — This book was one of the first popular books written about the social consequences of innumeracy. It's a quick read and will give you an excellent sense of the importance of changing perceptions regarding mathematics in your school.

*Designing Effective Mathematics Instruction: A Direct Instruction Approach* by M. Stein, J. Silbert, and D. Carnine (1997) — This is an indispensable book for teachers who need help with teaching mathematics on a very practical, day-to-day basis. If you have a teacher who is math-phobic, doesn't have an adequate mathematics background, or is working with a particularly challenging student, this is the book to have. Special education teachers swear by the book, but it will work for every child.

*The Learning Gap* by Harold W. Stevenson and James W. Stigler (1992) — This was one of the first books to illuminate the startling differences between Japanese and American mathematics classrooms. It is a highly informative and interesting book, well written for the popular audience.

## Problem-Solving Bowl

Organize a classroom, grade-level, or schoolwide problem-solving competition. Choose problems suitable for a range of grade levels (e.g., primary, intermediate, middle school, high school). This activity can be the culminating activity for a year-long schoolwide emphasis on problem-solving skills or can be held at intervals during a year when problem solving is a major goal.

## Observe Mathematics Instruction Daily

Observe mathematics instruction at some grade level in your school every single day. There is no substitute for knowing exactly what is going on in every classroom. You should be aware of the students who are having difficulties. Affirm those teachers who are effective and counsel with those who are having difficulties. Your mere presence in the classroom will affect achievement in a positive way (Andrews & Soder, 1987).

## Math Incentive Programs

Designing a math incentive program takes a little more creativity than coming up with a program that motivates students to read. When I was a principal, we started with a basic facts program, since the majority of our students did not have automaticity and fluency with their math facts. We called it Math Facts Super Bowl, held it in January when football fever gripped our community (the Chicago Bears were playing the Super Bowl), and challenged a school in a neighboring community to a paper-and-pencil competition. Representatives from each school developed the ground rules, and on the appointed date we held the test-off. Because we won the competition, the rival school's principal attended our awards' assembly and presented me with a T-shirt. After Math Facts, move on to problem solving.

## Parent Involvement

Explore ways to involve parents in their children's mathematical education. At *http://www.enc.org/focus/topics/family/index.htm* you will find links to a variety of resources designed to help parents become numerate right along with their children.

## Solve-a-Lot

To gain fluency and skill in problem solving, students must solve a lot of problems. They must gain confidence in their abilities to figure out difficult problems and have the opportunity to talk about problem solving with other students. Survey your teachers to determine how frequently they include solving word problems in their daily lessons. Check out how many and what kinds of examples and problems are included in your math program. If your goal is to create world-class problem solvers, your students must have daily opportunities to solve world-class problems.

## Principal's List

I knew the name and academic history of all of the target students (i.e., those students whose achievement was below grade level) in my school. When I observed in classrooms, I took special note of how and what these students were doing. I read interim reports sent to parents and signed off on their grade reports. More important, I focused on what teachers were doing to raise expectations, to offer special attention, and to make modifications in instruction to meet the needs of targeted students. I regularly asked teachers about students' progress. I talked with parents as well to make sure they were being kept informed. Target students sometimes had no one who was either able or willing to act as an advocate. When teachers knew that I cared, their expectations for these students increased.

## Evaluation for Mathematics Achievement

When you are writing those often-dreaded annual teacher evaluations, use them as an opportunity to focus on mathematics instruction. Commend teachers who are doing a good job by specifically noting the effective things they have done in their classrooms to contribute to the goal of raising mathematics achievement. Suggest ways of improving to those who are unsure of how to change what they are doing. What you highlight in the evaluation process will be discussed in the teachers' lounge. What gets noticed gets done!

## Math Book Discussion Group

Oprah isn't the only one who can motivate people to read books that she personally chooses. Form a book discussion group with your faculty. Instead of fiction, however, choose a book about math from your professional library. Stretch your mind and those of your faculty members. My first choice of a book for elementary teachers would be Liping Ma's *Knowing and Teaching Elementary Mathematics: Teachers' Understanding of Fundamental Mathematics in China and the United States* (1999). It examines the differences between Chinese and American teachers' approaches to teaching mathematics. I can imagine this book generating many interesting and somewhat heated discussions. For middle and high school teachers I would choose *Escalante: The Best Teacher in America,* the story of Jaime Escalante, the teacher who taught AP calculus at Garfield High School in East Los Angeles (Mathews, 1988).

## Math Mentors

Identify students with promise in mathematics and team them up with a community mentor. Arrange for job shadowing and occasional informal meetings to encourage students to continue taking higher math courses.

## Math and Science Career Day

Invite parents and community members to your school to talk about how they use mathematics in their careers (or about how necessary it was for their training and preparation). Health-care professionals, economists, veterinarians, surveyors, stockbrokers, actuaries, airline pilots, economists, and auto repair technicians are just a few folks to invite along with the traditional engineers, math teachers, and astronauts.

## Release Your Staff

One of our most effective programs for improving instruction was the periodic release of teachers individually or by grade level from their classroom responsibilities for one-half day. Teachers can use this time for many activities, any one of which has the potential to raise achievement. They can talk about each of their students' progress with the principal and the student-assistance team, meet with a math specialist to learn about a new strategy or method to teach problem solving, meet with other teachers at their grade level to plan a unit of study, or visit a colleague and observe a math lesson.

## Read About Math. Talk About Math. Do Math.

Conduct your own personal self-study program related to mathematics instruction. Become an expert. Tutor a child to gain firsthand experience regarding the challenges of math instruction. Teach your teachers. Talk to your teachers. Engage them in meaningful dialogue and discussion about how students learn math. Ask questions wherever you go. Find out if teachers have reasons for doing what they are doing. If you are an elementary principal, choose a key lesson topic (e.g., place value, subtraction with regrouping), determine when a teacher will be starting that unit with his/her classroom, then visit every day so that you can see the development and progression of the lesson. If you are a middle- or high school principal, do the same. Visit an algebra I class from the very first day of the semester. Do the homework; become a student in the classroom for a week or two. You will soon discover if instruction is clear and meaningful. You will also send a strong message to teachers and students in your school. Who knows, you may even learn something new!

## The Principal's Problem

Post a mathematics problem every day on the bulletin board outside of your office. Offer a nominal prize (pencil, coupon for the school bookstore or a local fast food restaurant, or a skip-your-homework pass) to the first student who arrives with the solution. Place a limit on the number of times one student can win a prize to give other students a chance. Encourage classroom teachers to use the problem as a classwide activity and give a perk to the first classroom to arrive at the correct answer.

## Stump the Teachers

From time to time gather a grade level of students together and challenge teams of teachers and students to compete against one another to find the correct answers to mathematics problems. The enthusiasm generated for mathematics will surprise you, as will the difficulty of the problems.

## Swarthmore Math Forum

The Math Forum is an on-line program funded in part by the National Science Foundation and hosted by Swarthmore College. There are discussion groups, problems of the week, Web units and lessons (the Dr. Math and Teacher2Teacher features mentioned earlier), and a collection of math resources by subject. You can access the Forum at *http://forum.swarthmore.edu/*.

## Math Accuracy and Time Help (Math) Skill Drills Program

The MATH Skill Drills program provides multiple copies of each drill for each level bound in six different books, designed so that most students should be able to complete the entire program by the end of sixth grade. Students progress at their own rate. When pupils meet the time and accuracy criteria for each sheet, they move on to the next level until they complete the book. Students graph their daily performance on individual progress charts. Book 1 begins with basic addition and subtraction, and by the time the students reach sixth grade they are covering decimals, fractions, percents, and geometric concepts. For more information, contact Lynn Hatfield at the Council for Exceptional Children, Ontario, Canada, (705) 324-2759.

## The Teaching Gap

The authors of *The Teaching Gap,* James W. Stigler and James Hiebert (1999) have designed a Web site focused on improving mathematics instruction. Teachers can participate in a discussion group and explore various aspects of the TIMSS video study, which prompted the writing of the book. Visit the site at *http://www.lessonlab.com/teaching-gap*.

### *The High School Mathematics Teachers' Basic Library*

Build a library of books for your high school mathematics teachers that will help them enhance students' problem-solving skills. Begin with these titles: *Problem-Solving Strategies for Efficient and Elegant Solutions* (Posamentier & Krulik, 1998); *The Art of Problem Solving: A Resource for Mathematics Teachers* (Posamentier & Schulz, 1996); and *Tips for the Mathematics Teacher: Research-Based Strategies to Help Students Learn* (Posamentier, Hartman, & Kaiser, 1998).

### *What Should We Teach and How Should We Teach It?*

*The Mathematics Framework for California Public Schools, Kindergarten Through Grade 12* is a gold mine of information for administrators and teachers. If you need a road map to help you raise mathematics achievement in your school, this document will be invaluable. Copies of the publication can be obtained by calling the sales office at (800) 995-4099.

### *IMACS*

The Institute for Mathematics and Computer Science is located in Broward County in south Florida. Visit their Web site at *www.imacs.org* to read more about this unique opportunity for talented mathematics students. The curriculum was developed by some of the finest mathematicians and educators from around the world. Sessions are held after school, on weekends, and during the summer months.

Writing *The Principal's Guide to Raising Mathematics Achievement* has been a challenging and enormously exciting experience for me. The research I have done for the book has put me in touch with mathematicians, educators, researchers, and parents around the country, all committed to helping our students become successful and competitive. In my opinion, there has never been a better time to be about the business of raising mathematics achievement. There are promising research results, public interest and support, and an enormous job to be done. I hope that you will rise to the challenge and lead your school to mathematical excellence.

If you have questions, comments, or success stories to share, please contact me at emcewan@azstarnet.com. If you are interested in scheduling a Raising Reading Achievement or Raising Mathematics Achievement workshop in your district or school, visit my Web site at *www.elainemcewan.com* to see available dates, then e-mail me your request.

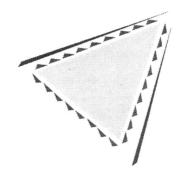

# References

Abt Associates. (1976). *Education as experimentation: A planned variation model (Vol. 3A)*. Cambridge, MA: Author.

Adelman, C. (1999, June). *Answers in the tool box: Academic intensity, attendance patterns, and bachelor's degree attainment*. Washington, DC: U.S. Department of Education, Office of Educational Research and Improvement. Retrieved November 1999 from the World Wide Web: http://www.ed.gov/pubs/Toolbox/

Allen, F. (1996, April). *A program for raising the level of student achievement in secondary school mathematics*. Retrieved November 1999 from the World Wide Web: http://www.mathematicallycorrect.com/allen.htm

Allen, F. (1997, February). *Address to the math department chairpersons of the West Chicago suburbs*. Lisle, IL.

American Association for the Advancement of Science. (1999). *Middle grades mathematics textbooks*. Washington, DC: Author. Retrieved November 1999 from the World Wide Web: http://www.project2061.org/matheval/index.htm

Anastasiow. N. J., Sibley, S. A., Leonhardt, T. M., & Borich, G. D. (1970). A comparison of guided discovery, discovery and didactic teaching of math to kindergarten poverty children. *American Educational Research Journal, 7*, 493–510.

Anderson, J. R., Reder, L. M. & Simon, H. A. (1995). *Applications and misapplications of cognitive psychology to mathematics education*. Pittsburgh: Carnegie Mellon University, Department of Psychology. Retrieved November 1999 from the World Wide Web: http://act.psy.cmu.edu/personal/ja/misapplied.html.

Anderson, L. (1980). Dimensions in classroom management derived from recent research. *Journal of Curriculum Studies, 12*, 343–356.

Andrews, R., & Soder, R. (1987, March). Principal leadership and student achievement. *Educational Leadership, 44*, 9–11.

Apelman, M. (1986). Working with teachers: The advisory approach. In K. Zumwalt, (Ed.) *Improving teaching* (pp. 115–129). Alexandria, VA: Association for Supervision and Curriculum Development.

Ashton, P. T., & Webb, R. B. (1986). *Making a difference: Teachers' sense of efficacy and student achievement*. New York: Longman.

Balow, I. (1964). Reading and computation ability as determinants of problem solving. *The Arithmetic Teacher, 11*, 18–22.

Battista, M.T. (1999, February). The mathematical miseducation of America's youth. *Phi Delta Kappan,* 424–433.

Beaton, A. E., Mullis, I. V. S., Martin, M. O., Gonzalez, E. J., Kelly, D. L., & Smith, T. A. (1996, November). *Mathematics achievement in the middle school years: IEA's third international mathematics and science study (TIMSS)*. Chestnut Hill, MA: International Association for the Evaluation of Educational Achievement. Retrieved November 1999 from the World Wide Web: http://www.timss.be.edu/TIMSSPublications.html in portable document file (PDF) format.

Beers, D. E. (1984). *School-based management.* Paper presented at National Convention of Elementary School Principals, New Orleans.

Bell, J. (1999, August 25). Parents to file lawsuit today. *Plano Star Courier,* 1.

Benezet, L. P. (1935a). The story of an experiment: The teaching of arithmetic. *Journal of the National Education Association, 24*(8), 241–244.

Benezet, L. P. (1935b). The story of an experiment: The teaching of arithmetic II. *Journal of the National Education Association, 24*(9), 301–303.

Benezet, L. P. (1936). The story of an experiment: The teaching of arithmetic III. *Journal of the National Education Association, 25*(1), 7–8.

Benjamin, G. R. (1997). *Japanese lessons: A year in a Japanese school through the eyes of an American anthropologist and her children.* New York: New York University Press.

Black, P., & Atkins, J. M. (1996). Changing the subject: Innovations in science, mathematics, and technology education. London: Routledge & Kegan Paul.

Blakeslee, S. (1999, May 11). Brain's math machine traced to 2 circuits. *New York Times,* p. P9.

Bloom, B. (1980). The state of research on selected alterable variables in education. Chicago: University of Chicago Department of Education.

Bock, G., Stebbins, L., & Proper, E. 1977. *Education as experimentation: A planned variation model, Volume IV-B.* Cambridge, MA: Abt Associates.

Boser, U. (1999, June 23). Study finds mismatch between California standards and assessments. *Education Week,* 10.

Bransford, J., & The Cognition and Technology Group of Vanderbilt University. (1993). The Jasper series: Theoretical foundations and data on problem solving and transfer. In L. A. Penner, G. M. Batsche, H. M. Knoff, & D. L. Nelson (Eds.), *The challenge in mathematics and science education: Psychology's response* (pp. 113–152). Washington, DC: American Psychological Association.

Briars, D., & Siegler, R. S. (1984). A featural analysis of preschoolers' counting knowledge. *Developmental Psychology, 22,* 723–742.

Briars, D. J., & Larkin, J. H. (1984). An integrated model of skill in solving elementary word problems. *Cognition and Instruction, 1,* 245–296.

Bright, G. W., Harvey, J. G., & Wheeler, M. M. (1981). Varying manipulative game constraints. *Journal of Educational Research, 74,* 347–351.

Britton, B. K., Woodward, A., & Binkley, M. (Eds.). (1993). *Learning from textbooks: Theory and practice.* Hillsdale, NJ: Lawrence Erlbaum.

Brophy, J. (1979). Teacher behavior and its effects. *Journal of Educational Psychology, 71,* 733–750.

Brown, R. G., Dolciani, M. P., Sorgenfrey, R. H., Cole, W. L., Campbell, C., & Piper, J. M. (1994). *Algebra: Structure and method. Book I.* New York: McDougal Littell/Houghton Mifflin.

Burns, M. (1998). *Math: Facing an American phobia.* New York: Math Solutions Publications.

Business Coalition for Education Reform. (1999). Business cares about math and science. Section Two. In *The formula for success: A business leader's guide to supporting math and science achievement.* Author. Retrieved November, 1999 from the World Wide Web: http://www.bcer.org/times/index.cfm

Butterworth, B. (1999). *What counts: How every brain is hardwired for math.* New York: The Free Press.

California Department of Education. (1999). *Mathematics framework for California public schools: Kindergarten through grade twelve.* Sacramento, CA: Author.

California State Board of Education. (1999). *Mathematics content standards for California public schools: Kindergarten through grade twelve,* Author. Retrieved November 1999 from the World Wide Web: http://www.cde.ca.gov/board/mcs_intro.html in portable document file (PDF) format.

Campbell, D. T., & Stanley, J. C. (1963). *Experimental and quasi-experimental designs for research.* Boston: Houghton Mifflin.

Carnine, D. (1993, December 8). Facts over fads. *Education Week,* 40.

Carter, S. C. (1999). *No excuses: Seven principals of low-income schools who set the standard for high achievement.* Washington, DC: The Heritage Foundation.

Castro, G. (1997). In *Mathematics equals opportunity: White paper prepared for U.S. Secretary of Education Richard W. Riley.* [On-line]. Washington, DC: Department of Education. Retrieved November 1999 from the World Wide Web: http://165.224.220.67/pubs/math/

Center for the Education and Study of Diverse Populations. *New Mexico standards for mathematics: Content standard 1.* Rio Rancho, NM: New Mexico Highlands University. Retrieved November 1999 from the World Wide Web: http://www.cesdp.nmhu.edu/standards/content/math/stan_ben/index.htm

Charles, R. I., Thompson, A. G., Garland, T. H., & Dossey, J. A. (1997). *Focus on algebra: An integrated approach.* Reading, MA: Scott Foresman/Addison-Wesley.

Clopton, P., Bishop, W., & Klein, D. (1998). Statewide mathematics assessment in Texas. Retrieved November 1999 from the World Wide Web: http://www.mathematicallycorrect.com/lonestar.htm

Clopton, P., McKeown, E. H., McKeown, M., & Clopton, J. (1998). *Mathematically correct algebra I reviews* [On-line]. Retrieved November 1999 from the World Wide Web: http://www.mathematicallycorrect.com/algebra.htm

Clopton, P., McKeown, E., McKeown, M., & Clopton, J. (1999). *Mathematics program reviews for grades 2, 5, and 7* [On-line]. Retrieved November 1999 from the World Wide Web: http://www.mathematicallycorrect.com/books.htm

Cobb, P., Yackel, E., & Wood, T. (1992). A constructivist alternative to the representational view of mind in mathematics education. *Journal for Research in Mathematics Education, 23,* 2–33.

Cockcroft, W. H. (1982). *Mathematics counts: Report of the Committee of Inquiry into the Training of Mathematics in Schools.* London: HMSO.

Coffey, D. (1999, August 20). Education progress just in time. *Oak Ridger* (Oak Ridge, TN), p. 6A.

Coleman, J. (1966). *Equality of educational opportunity.* Washington, DC: U.S. Department of Health, Education and Welfare, Office of Education.

Colvin, R. (1999a). Math wars: Tradition vs. real-world applications. School Administrator [On-line]. American Association of School Administrators. Retrieved November 1999 from the World Wide Web: http://www.aasa.org/SA/jan9902.htm

Colvin, R. (1999b, September 17). Experts attack math teaching programs. *Los Angeles Times,* p. A3.

Comenius, J. A. (1632/1967). *The great didactic.* (M.W. Keating, Trans.). New York: Russell & Russell. (Original work published 1632)

Concerned Parents of Reading, MA. *Information about "new new math."* Author. Retrieved November 1999 from the World Wide Web: http://member.aol.com/rlmandell/CPR/start.html

Cook, T. D., & Campbell, D. T. (1979). *Quasi-experimentation: Design and analysis issues for field studies.* Chicago: Rand McNally.

Cooper, G., & Sweller, J. (1987). Effects of schema acquisition and rule automation on mathematical problem-solving transfer. *Journal of Educational Psychology, 79* 347–362.

Corella, H. R. & Tapia, S. T. (1999, November 16). Graduation test shows students have work ahead. *Arizona Daily Start,* p. 1A.

Creative Publications Inc. (1978). *Didactics and mathematics: The art and science of learning and teaching mathematics.* Palo Alto, CA: Author.

Curcio, F. (1999, February). On my mind: Dispelling myths about reform in school mathematics. *Mathematics Teaching in the Middle School.* [On-line]. Retrieved November 1999 from the World Wide Web: http://www.nctm.org/mtms/1999/02/onmymind.htm

Dabbs, J. M. (1982). Making things visible. In J. Van Maane, J. M. Dabbs, & R. R. Faulker (Eds.), *Varieties of qualitative research* (pp. 31–63). Beverly Hills, CA: Sage.

Dantzig, T. (1954). *Number, The language of science.* Garden City, NJ: Doubleday.

Darling-Hammond, L., Ancess, J., & Falk, B. (1995). *Authentic assessment in action: Studies of schools and students at work.* New York: Teachers College Press.

Dawkins, R. (1986). *The blind watchmaker.* New York: Norton.

DeCorte, E., & Verschaffel, L. (1991). Some factors influencing the solution of addition and subtraction word problems. In K. Durkin & B. Shire (Eds.), *Language in mathematical education* (pp. 117–130). Philadelphia: Open University Press.

Dehaene, S. (1997). *The number sense.* New York: Oxford University Press.

Dehaene, S., Spelke, E., Pinel, P., Stanescu, R., & Tsivkin, S. (1999, May 7). Sources of mathematical thinking: Behavioral and brain-imaging evidence. *Science 284,* 970–974.

Dewdney, A. K. (1993). *200% of nothing: An eye-opening tour through the twists and turns of math abuse and innumeracy.* New York: John Wiley.

DeWeese, T. (1999, August 2). The death of math in America. *The DeWeese Report* [On-line]. American Policy Center. Retrieved November 1999 from the World Wide Web: http://www.americanpolicy.org/plate.main/death.html

Diens, Z. P. (1970). Some basic processes involved in mathematics learning. In R. Ashlock and W. L. Herman (Eds.), *Current research in elementary school mathematics* (pp. 51–54). New York: Macmillan.

Direct Instruction Consumer Reports. (1996). *Evaluations of general education mathematics programs* [On-line]. Author. Retrieved February 9, 2000, from the World Wide Web: http://darkwing.uoregon.edu/~adiep/math.htm

Dixon, R. C., Carnine, D. W., Lee, D., Wallin, J., & Chard, D. (1998a). *Report to the California State Board of Education: Review of high quality experimental mathematics research.* [On-line]. Eugene, OR:

National Center to Improve the Tools of Educators, University of Oregon. Retrieved November 1999 from the World Wide Web: http://idea.uoregon.edu/~ncite/documents/math/math.html

Dixon, R.C., Carnine, D.W., Lee, D., Wallin, J. Chard, D. (1998b). Executive summary "at a glance" [On-line]. Eugene, OR: National Center to Improve the Tools of Educators, University of Oregon. Retrieved November 1999 from the World Wide Web: http://idea.uoregon.edu/7Encite/documents/math

Donahue, P. L., Voelkl, K. E., Campbell, J. R., & Mazzeo, J. (1999, March). *Report card for the nation and the states*. National Assessment of Educational Progress, 1998 Reading. Washington, DC: U.S. Department of Education, Office of Educational Research and Improvement, National Center for Education Statistics. 199–500.

Dossey, J. L., Lindquist, M., & Chamber, M. M. (1988). *The mathematics report card: Are we measuring up? Trends and achievement based on the 1986 national assessment*. Princeton, NJ: Educational Testing Service.

Drum, R. L., & Petty, W. G. (1999). Teaching the values of coins. *Teaching Children Mathematics, 5*(5), 264–268.

Durkin, K., & Shire, B. (1991). Lexical ambiguity in mathematical contexts. In K. Durkin & B. Shire (Eds.), *Language in mathematical education* (pp. 71–84). Philadelphia: Open University Press.

Ebeling, D. (1974, June). The ability of sixth grade students to associate mathematical terms with related algorithms. *Dissertation Abstracts, Vol. 34A*, pp. 7514–7515. Bloomington, IN: Indiana University.

Ebrahimi, H. (1999, May 26). Early math: Doing the greatest good for the greatest number. *Education Week*, pp. 31, 48.

Education Development Center. K–12 Mathematics Curriculum Center. (1999, January). *Curriculum summaries* [On-line]. Author. Retrieved November 1999 from the World Wide Web: http://www.edc.org/mcc

Educational Testing Service. (1996). *The comprehensive needs assessment: A basis for making schoolwide decisions*. Tucker, GA:.Author.

Eliot, C. W. (1961). Shortening and enriching the grammar school course. In E. A. Krug (Ed.), *Charles W. Eliot and popular education* (pp. 52–53). New York: Teachers College Press. (Original work published 1892)

Ellis, A. K., & Fouts, J. T. (1997). *Research on educational innovations* (2nd ed.). West Larchmont, NY: Eye on Education.

Emmer, E. T., & Evertson, C. M. (1981). *Effective management at the beginning of the school year in junior high classes* (Report No. 6108). Austin: University of Texas, Research and Development Center of Teacher Education.

Engelhardt, J. M., Ashlock, R. B., & Wiebe, J. H. (1984). *Helping children understand and use numerals*. Boston: Allyn and Bacon.

English, F. (1992). *Deciding what to teach and test: Developing, aligning, and auditing the curriculum*. Thousand Oaks, CA: Corwin.

Ericsson, K. A., Krampe, R. T., & Tesche-Römer, C. (1993). The role of deliberate practice in the acquisition of expert performance. *Psychological Review, 100*, 363–406.

Evertson, C. M. (1982). Differences in instructional activities in higher and lower achieving junior high English and mathematics classrooms. *Elementary School Journal, 82*, 329–351.

Finn, C. (1993, January 20). What if those math standards are wrong? *Education Week* [On-line]. Retrieved November 1999 from the World Wide Web: http://www.edweek.org

Fleener, M. J., DuPreee, G. N., & Craven, L. D. (1997, September). Exploring and changing visions of mathematics teaching and learning: What do students think? *Mathematics Teaching in the Middle School, 3*(1), 40–43.

Fleener, M. J., & Reynolds, A. (1994). The relationship between preservice teachers' metaphors for mathematics learning and Habermasian interests. In *Proceedings of the Sixteenth Annual Meeting of Psychology in Mathematics Education-National (PME-NA)* 247–253. Baton Rouge, LA: Louisiana State University.

Fullan, M. G. (1992). Visions that blind. *Educational Leadership, 49*, 19–20.

Fullan, M. G. (1994). *Change forces: Probing the depths of educational reform*. New York: Falmer Press.

Fullan, M., & Miles, M. (1992). Getting reform right: What works and what doesn't. *Phi Delta Kappan, 73*(10) 745–752.

Fuson, K. C. (1988). *Children's counting and concepts of number*. New York: Springer-Verlag.

Gardner, Martin. (1998, September 24). The new new math. *New York Review of Books*, 9–12.

Geary, D. (1994). *Children's mathematical development: Research and practical applications*. Washington, DC: American Psychological Association.

Geary, D., & Widaman, K. F. (1992). Numerical cognition: On the convergence of componential and psychometric models. *Intelligence, 16*, 47–80.

Gelernter, D. (1998, May 21). Put down that calculator, stupid. [On-line]. *New York Post.* Retrieved November 1999 from the World Wide Web: http://www.nypostonline.com/commentary/2735.htm

Gelman, S. (1978). A context for learning: Concept development in preschool children. *Dialogue on Early Childhood Science, Mathematics, and Technology Education.* American Association for the Advancement of Science. Retrieved November 1999 from the World Wide Web: http://project 2061.aaas.org/newsinfo/earlychild/context/gelman.htm

Gelman, S., & Gallistel, C. R. (1978). *The child's understanding of number.* Cambridge, MA: Harvard University Press.

Ginsburg, H. P. (1989). *Children's arithmetic: How they learn it and how you teach it* (2nd ed.). Austin, TX: Pro-Ed.

Ginsburg, H. P., & Baron, J. (1993). Cognition: Young children's construction of mathematics. In R.J. Jensen & S. Wagner (Eds.) *Early childhood mathematics* (pp. 3–21). New York: Macmillan.

Glass, G., & McGaw, B. (1981). *Meta-analysis in social research.* Thousand Oaks, CA: Sage Publications.

Goldman, M. (1998, May 6). Time to solve the math education equation. *Education Week,* 40, 56.

Goldring, E. B., & Rallis, S. F. (1993). *Principals of dynamic schools: Taking charge of change.* Newbury Park, CA: Corwin.

Goldsmith, L. T., Mark, J., & Kantrov, I. (1999). *Choosing a standards-based mathematics curriculum.* Portsmouth, NH: Heinemann Education.

Good, R. (1979). Children's abilities with the four basic arithmetic operations in grades K–2. *Science and Mathematics,* 79(2), 93–98.

Good, T. L., Grouws, D. A., & Ebmeier, H. (1983). *Active mathematics teaching.* New York: Longman.

Griffin, S. A., & Case, R. (1997). Rethinking the primary school math curriculum: An approach based on cognitive science. *Issues in Education,* 3(1), 1–49.

Griffin, S. A., Case, R., & Siegler, R. S. (1994). Rightstart: Providing the central conceptual prerequisites for first formal learning of arithmetic to students at risk for school failure. In K. McGilly (Ed.), *Classroom lessons: Integrating cognitive theory and classroom practice* (pp. 25–49). Cambridge, MA: The MIT Press.

Grossen, B. (1996, Fall). Making research serve the profession. *American Educator,* 20(3), 7–8, 22–27.

Grouws, D. A. (1992). (Ed.). *Handbook of research on mathematics teaching and learning.* Hillsdale, NJ: Lawrence Erlbaum.

Hall, S. L., & Moats, L. C. (1998). *Straight talk about reading.* New York, Contemporary Books.

Hanna, G. (1999). Orleans-Hanna Algebra Prognosis Test (3rd ed.). New York: Harcourt Inc.

Harcourt Inc. (1999). *Stanford Diagnostic Mathematics Test* (3rd ed.). New York: Author.

Harrison, B., Brindley, S., & Bye, M. P. (1989). Allowing for student cognitive levels in the teaching of fractions and rations. *Journal for Research in Mathematics Education,* 20(3), 288–300.

Harrison, C. R., Killion, J. P., & Mitchell, J. E. (1989). Site-based management: The realities of implementation. *Educational Leadership,* 46(8), 55–58.

Hawkes, M., Kimmelman, P., & Kroeze, D. (1997, September). Becoming "first in the world" in math and science: Moving high expectations and promising practices to scale. *Phi Delta Kappan,* 30–33.

Hayes, J. R. (1985). Three problems in teaching general skills. In J. Segal, S. Chipman, & R. Glaser (Eds.), *Thinking and learning skills, vol.2* (pp. 391–405). Hillsdale, NJ: Lawrence Erlbaum.

Haylock, D. (1995). *Mathematics explained for primary teachers.* London: Paul Chapman Publishing Ltd.

Heck, R., Larson, T., & Marcoulides, G. (1990). Principal instructional leadership and school achievement: Validation of a causal model. Educational Administration Quarterly, 26, 94–125.

Heck, R., Marcoulides, G., & Lang, P. (1991). Principal instructional leadership and school achievement: The application of discriminant techniques. *School Effectiveness and School Improvement, 2,* 115-135.

Hiebert, J. (1986). (Ed.). *Conceptual and procedural knowledge: The case of mathematics.* Hillsdale, NJ: Lawrence Erlbaum.

Hiebert, J. (1999, January). Relationships betweeen research and the NCTM standards. *Journal for Research in Mathematics Education,* 30(1), 3–19.

Hiebert, J., & Carpenter, T. P. (1992). Learning and teaching with understanding. In D. A. Grouw, (Ed.), *Handbook on research in mathematics and teaching and learning* (pp. 65–97). New York: Macmillan.

Hirsch, E. D. (1996). *The schools we need and why we don't have them.* New York: Doubleday.

Hoff, D. J. (1998, November 4). Math council again mulling its standards. *Education Week,* 16.

Hughes, M. (1986). *Children and number: Difficulties in learning mathematics.* Oxford, United Kingdom: Basil Blackwell.

Illinois School Report Card. (1998). Glencoe School District 35 [On-line]. Retrieved November 1999 from the World Wide Web: http:chicagotribune.com

International Association for the Evaluation of Educational Achievement. (1997). *TIMSS achievement items*. Chestnut Hill: MA: Author. Retrieved November 1999 from the World Wide Web: http://timss.be.edu in portable document file (PDF) format.

Jackson, G. B. (1976, April). *Methods for reviewing and integrating research in the social sciences*. Final Report to the National Science Foundation for Grant No. DIS76-20309. Washington, DC: Social Research Group, George Washington University.

Japan Society of Mathematical Education. (1990, January). *Mathematics program in Japan: Kindergarten to upper secondary school*. Tokyo, Japan: Author. Reprinted by the U.S. Department of Education with permission, 1999.

Jennings, M. M. (1996, December 17). MTV math doesn't add up. *Wall Street Journal*, p. A22.

Jonassen, D. H., Beissner, K., & Yacci, M. (1993). *Structural knowledge*. Hillsdale, NJ: Lawrence Erlbaum.

Kamii, C. (1982). *Number in preschool and kindergarten: educational implications of Piaget's theory*. Washington, DC: National Association for the Education of Young Children.

Kamii, C. (1985). *Young children reinvent arithmetic: Implications of Piaget's theory*. New York: Teachers College Press.

Kantrowitz, B. (1997, December 15). Subtracting the new math. *Newsweek*, 62.

Kasten, M., & Howe, R. W. (1988). Students at risk in mathematics: Implications for elementary schools. *ERIC/SMEAC Mathematics Education Digest No. 2*. ERIC Accession No. ED321971

Kearns, D. (1989, December 17). Improving the workforce: Competitiveness begins at school. *New York Times* Section 3, 2.

Kilpatrick, J. (1988). Editorial. *Journal for Research in Mathematics Education, 19*(4), 274.

Kohn, A. (1986). *No contest: The case against competition*. Boston: Houghton Mifflin.

Kolata, G. (1997). Understanding the news. In L. A. Steen, (Ed.), *Why numbers count: Quantitative literacy for tomorrow's America* (pp. 23–29). New York: The College Board.

Kollars, D. (1999, June 25). City schools improve in statewise reading, math tests. *Sacramento Bee*, [On-line]. Retrieved June 26, 1999, from the World Wide Web: http://www.sacbee.com

Kremer, R. (1998, May). Feeling good about math. *Brainstorm Magazine* [On-line]. Retrieved January 2000 from the World Wide Web: http://www.oregoneducation.org/math/feeling.htm

Kumon, T. (1991, April 1). It should all begin with a song. *Time*, 55.

Labaree, D. F. (1999, May 19). The chronic failure of curriculum reform. *Education Week*, 42–43.

Lackner, L. M. (1972). Teaching of limit and derivative concepts in beginning calculus by combinations of inductive and deductive methods. *Journal of Experimental Education, 40*, 51–56.

Lally, K., & Price, D. M. (1997, November 3). The brain reads sound by sound. *Baltimore Sun* [On-line]. Retrieved November 8, 1997, from the World Wide Web: http://www.sunspot.net/

Lampert, M. (1990). When the problem is not the question and the solution is not the answer: Mathematical knowing and teaching. *American Educational Research Journal, 27*, 29–63.

Latham, G. (1988, September). The birth and death cycles of educational innovations. *Principal*, 41–43.

Learning First Alliance. (1998, November). *Every child mathematically proficient: An action plan of the Learning First Alliance*. Washington, DC: Author.

Leinwand, S. (1994, February 9). It's time to abandon computational algorithms. *Education Week* [On-line]. Retrieved November 1999 from the World Wide Web: http://www.educationweek.org

Lennes, N. J. (1908). Modern tendencies in the teaching of algebra. *The Mathematics Teacher, 1*, 94–104.

Leo, J. (1997, May 26). On society: That so-called Pythagoras. *U.S. News & World Report*, 14.

Levin, J. R., & Mayer, R. E. (1993). Understanding illustrations in text. In B. Britton, A. Woodward, & M. Binkley (Eds.), *Learning from textbooks: Theory and practice* (pp. 95–113). Hillsdale, NJ: Lawrence Erlbaum.

Lewis, C., & Tsuchida, I. (1997). Planned educational change in Japan: The shift to student-centered elementary science. *Journal of Educational Policy, 12*, 313–331.

Lewis, C., & Tsuchida, I. (1998). A lesson is like a swiftly flowing river: How research lessons improve Japanese education. *American Educator, 22*(4), 12–17, 50–52.

Lionni, L. (1971). *Leo, the late bloomer*. New York: Windmill Books.

Lortie, D. (1975). *Schoolteacher*. Chicago: University of Chicago Press.

Louis, K., & Miles, M. (1990). Improving the urban high school. New York: Teachers College Press.

Loveless, T. (1997, October 15). The second great math rebellion. *Education Week* [On-line]. Retrieved November 1999 from the World Wide Web: http://www.edweek.org

Lukhele, R., Thissen, D., & Wainer, H. (1994). On the relative values of multiple-choice, constructed response, and examinee-selected items on two achievement tests. *Journal of Educational Measurement, 31*(3), 234–250.

Ma, L. (1999). *Knowing and teaching elementary mathematics: Teachers' understanding of fundamental mathematics in China and the United States*. Mahwah, NJ: Lawrence Erlbaum.

Mathematically Correct. (1997). *Mission statement.* Retrieved November 1999 from the World Wide Web: http://www.mathematicallycorrect.com

Mathews, J. (1988). *Escalante: The best teacher in America.* New York: Henry Holt.

Maurer, S. B. (1998). What is an algorithm? What is an answer? In L. J. Morrow & M. J. Kenney (Eds.). *The teaching and learning of algorithms in school mathematics: 1998 yearbook.* (pp. 21–31). Reston, VA: National Council of Teachers of Mathematics.

Maxim, G. W. (1989). Developing preschool mathematical concepts. *Arithmetic Teacher, 37*(4), 36–41.

Mayer, R. (1982). Memory for algebra story problems. *Journal of Educational Psychology, 74,* 199–216.

Mayer, R. E. (1987). *Educational psychology: A cognitive approach.* New York: HarperCollins.

Mayer, R. E. (1992). *Thinking, problem solving, cognition* (2nd ed.). New York: Freeman.

Mayer, R. E. (1993). Illustrations that instruct. In R. Glaser (Ed.), *Advances in instructional psychology, Vol. 4* (pp. 253–284). Hillsdale, NJ: Lawrence Erlbaum.

Mayer, R. E., Sims, V., & Tajika, H. (1995, Summer). A comparison of how textbooks teach mathematical problem solving in Japan and the United States. *American Association of Research Journal 32*(2), 443–460.

McArthur, D. Mathematics reform in theory and practice, and its implications for DoD students [On-line]. Author. Retrieved November 1999 from the World Wide Web: http://intres.com/math/McArthurAbstract.htm

McDaniel, M. A., & Schlager, M. S. (1990). Discovery learning and transfer of problem-solving skills. *Cognition and Instruction, 7*(2), 129–159.

McEwan, E. K. (1997). *Leading your team to excellence: How to make quality decisions.* Thousand Oaks, CA: Corwin Press.

McEwan, E. K. (1998a). *The principal's guide to raising reading achievement.* Thousand Oaks, CA: Corwin.

McEwan, E. K. (1998b). *Seven steps to effective instructional leadership.* Thousand Oaks, CA: Corwin.

Michigan Department of Education. (1998). *Overview of mathematics content standards. Strand 111.3 Inference and prediction.* [On-line]. Lansing, MI. Author. Retrieved November 1999 from the World Wide Web: http://cdp.mde.state.mi.us/MCF/ContentStandards/Mathematics/default.html

Miller, D. W. (1999, 6 August). The black hole of education research. *The Chronicle of Higher Education,* A1718.

Miller, K. F., & Stigler, J. W. (1987). Counting in Chinese: Cultural variation in a basic skill. *Cognitive Development, 2,* 279–305.

Mingus, T. Y., & Grassl, R. M. (1998). Algorithmic and recursive thinking: Current beliefs and their implications for the future. In L. J. Morrow & M. J. Kenney (Eds.), *The teaching and learning of algorithms in school mathematics: 1998 yearbook* (pp. 32–43). Reston, VA: National Council of Teachers of Mathematics.

Moody, W. B., Abell, R., & Bausell, R. B. (1971). The effect of activity-oriented instruction upon original learning, transfer, and retention. *Journal for Research in Mathematics Education, 2,* 207–212.

Mullis, I. V. S., Martin, M. O., Beaton, A. E., Gonzalez, E. J., Kelly, D. L., & Smith, T. A. (1997, June). *Mathematics achievement in the primary school years: IEA's third international mathematics and science study (TIMSS)* [On-line]. Chestnut Hill, MA: International Association for the Evaluation of Educational Achievement. Retrieved November 1999 from the World Wide Web: http://www.csteep.bc.edu/timss in portable document file (PDF) format.

Mullis, I. V. S., Martin, M. O., Beaton, A. E., Gonzalez, E. J., Kelly, D. L., & Smith, T. A. (1998, February). *Mathematics and science achievement in the final year of secondary school: IEA's third international mathematics and science study (TIMSS)* [On-line]. Chestnut Hill: MA: International Association for the Evaluation of Educational Achievement. Retrieved November 1999 from the World Wide Web: http://www.csteep.bc.edu/timss in portable document file (PDF) format.

Muth, K. D. (1984). Solving arithmetic word problems: Role of reading and computational skills. *Journal of Educational Psychology, 76,* 205–210.

National Center on the Educational Quality of the Workforce. (1995). *The other shoe: Education's contribution to the productivity of establishments.* Philadelphia: University of Pennsylvania.

National Center to Improve the Tools of Educators (1997). *A handbook for creating smart schools* [On-line]. Author. Retrieved June 1998 from the World Wide Web: http://darkwing.uoregon.edu/ncite/smart.htm

National Council of Teachers of Mathematics. (1980). *Agenda for action.* Reston: VA: Author.

National Council of Teachers of Mathematics. (1989). *Curriculum and evaluation standards for school mathematics.* Reston, VA: Author.

National Council of Teachers of Mathematics. (1998, October). *Principles and standards for school mathematics: Discussion draft.* Reston, VA: Author.

National Council of Teachers of Mathematics. (1998, October). *Principles and standards for school mathematics: Discussion draft.* Reston, VA: Author.

National Council of Teachers of Mathematics' Research Advisory Committee. (1988) NCTM curriculum and evaluation standards for school mathematics: Responses from the research community. *Journal for Research in Mathematics Education, 19*(4), 338–344.

National Research Council. (1989). *Everybody counts: A report to the nation on the future of mathematics.* Washington, DC: National Academy Press.

Nevo, D. (1991, October). *An evaluation-minded school: Developing internal evaluation systems.* Paper presented at the annual meeting of the American Evaluation Association, Chicago.

New Jersey State Board of Education. (1997). *New Jersey mathematics curriculum framework: Geometry and spatial sense.* [On-line]. Retrieved November 1999 from the World Wide Web: http://dimacs.rutgers.edu/nj_math_coalition/framework.html in portable document file (PDF) format.

Newmann, F. M., Lopez, G., & Bryk, A. S. (1998, October). *The quality of intellectual work in Chicago schools: A baseline report.* Chicago: Consortium on Chicago School Research.

*New York Times.* (1993, September 1). Rejecting Barbie, doll maker gains, p. D1. New York: Author.

Northwest Regional Educational Laboratory. (1984). *Effective schooling practices: A research synthesis.* Portland, OR: Author.

Novick, L. R. (1992). The role of expertise in solving arithmetic and algebra word problems by analogy. In J. I. D. Campbell (Ed.), *The nature and origins of mathematical skills* (pp. 155–188). Amsterdam: North-Holland.

O'Brien, T. C. (1999, February). Parrot math. *Phi Delta Kappan 2.*

Oklahoma State Department of Education. (1999). *Priority academic student skills for mathematics.* [On-line]. Oklahoma City: Author. Retrieved November 1999 http://www.sde.state.ok.us/acrob/pass/math/pdf in portable document file (PDF) format.

Olander, H. T., & Robertson, H. C. (1973). The effectiveness of discovery and expository methods in the teaching of fourth-grade mathematics. *Journal for Research in Mathematics Education, 4,* 33–44.

Open Letter to United States Secretary of Education, Richard Riley. (1999, November 18). *Washington Post,* p. A5.

Palmaffy, T. (1997, November). See Dick flunk. *Policy Review* [On-line]. Retrieved December 1997 from the World Wide Web: http://www.policyreview.com/heritage/p_review/nov97/flun

Pappas, T. (1994). *The magic of mathematics: Discovering the spell of mathematics.* San Carlos, CA: Wide World Publishing/Tetra.

Parker, G. M. (1990). *Team players and teamwork.* San Francisco: Jossey-Bass.

Pasnak, R., Hansbarger, A., Dodson, S. L., Hart, J. B., & Blaha, J. (1996). Differential results of instruction at the preoperational/concrete operational transition. *Psychology in the schools, 33*(1), 70–83.

Paulos, J. A. (1988). *Innumeracy: Mathematical illiteracy and its consequences.* New York: Hill & Wang.

Pavan, B. N. (1992, October). The benefits of nongraded schools. *Educational Leadership, 50*(2), 22-26.

Pcholko, A. S., Bantova, M. A., Moro, M.. I., & Pyshkalo, A. M. (1992). *Russian grade 3 mathematics.* (Robert H. Silverman, Trans.). Chicago: The University of Chicago School Mathematics Project. (Original work published 1978)

Phi Delta Kappa. (1980). *Why do some urban schools succeed?* Bloomington, IN: Author.

Piaget, J. (1952). *The child's conception of number.* London: Routledge & Paul.

Piaget, J. (1953). How children form mathematical concepts. *Scientific American, 189* (5), 74–79.

Piaget, J. (1973). Comments on mathematical education. In A. G. Howson (Ed.), *Developments in mathematical education: Proceedings of the Second International Congress on Mathematical Education.* Cambridge, MA: Cambridge University Press.

Policy Studies Associates. (1998, October). *An idea book on planning: Vol. 1.* Washington, DC: U.S. Department of Education.

Posamentier, A. S., Hartman, H. J., & Kaiser, C. (1998). *Tips for the mathematics teacher: Research-based strategies to help students learn.* Thousand Oaks, CA: Corwin.

Posamentier, A. S., & Krulik, S. (1998). *Problem-solving strategies for efficient and elegant solutions.* Thousand Oaks, CA: Corwin.

Posamentier, A. S., & Schulz, W. (1996). *The art of problem solving: A resource for mathematics teachers.* Thousand Oaks, CA: Corwin.

Posamentier, A. S., & Schulz, W. (1998). *Problem-solving strategies for efficient and elegant solutions.* Thousand Oaks, CA: Corwin.

Raimi, R. A., & Braden, L. S. (1998, March). *State mathematics standards: An appraisal of math standards in 46 states, the District of Columbia, and Japan* [On-line]. Thomas B. Fordham Foundation. Retrieved November 1999 from the World Wide Web http://www.edexcellence.net/ in portable document file (PDF) format.

Rathmell, E. C. (1975). [What upper grade students understand about number.] Unpublished raw data.

Ratnesar, R. (1997, August 17). This is math? *Time*, 66–67.

Reed, S. K. (1999). *Word problems: Research and curriculum reform*. Mahwah, NJ: Lawrence Erlbaum.

Resnick, L. B. (1983). A developmental theory of number understanding. In H. P. Ginsburg (Ed.), *The development of mathematical thinking* (pp. 110–151). New York: Academic Press.

Resnick, L. B. (1999, June 16). Making America smarter. *Education Week*, 38–40.

Rhode Island Department of Education. (1996). *Rhode Island K–12 math standards: Problem solving, grades 11–12* [On-line]. Providence, RI: Author. Retrieved November 1999 from the World Wide Web: http://instruct.ride.ri.net/doehome/MATHCHRT.html

RMC Research Corporation. (1995). *Schoolwide programs: A planning manual*. Portland, OR: Author.

Rosenshine, B. (1983). Teaching functions in instructional programs. *Elementary School Journal, 83* (4), 427–452.

Rutter, M., Maughan, B., Mortimore, P., & Ouston, J. (1979). *Fifteen thousand hours*. Cambridge, MA: Harvard University Press.

Sanders, W. L., & Rivers, J. C. (1996, November). *Cumulative and residual effects of teachers on future student academic achievement*. Knoxville: University of Tennessee Value Added Research and Assessment Center.

Sanders, W. L., Saxton, A. M., & Horn, S. P. (1997). The Tennessee Value-Added Assessment System: A quantitative, outcomes-based approach to educational assessment. In J. Millman (Ed.), *Grading teachers, grading schools: Is student achievement a valid evaluation measure?* (pp. 137–162). Thousand Oaks, CA: Corwin.

Santayana, G. (1982). The life of reason: Vol. 1. Reason in common sense. In J. Bartlett, (Ed.), *Bartlett's familiar quotes* (15th ed.). Boston: Little, Brown. (Original work published 1905–1906)

Saphier, J., & Gower, R. (1987). *The skillful teacher: Building your teaching skills*. Carlisle, MA: Research for Better Teaching.

Sarason, S. (1990). *The predictable future of educational reform: Can we change course before it's too late?* San Francisco: Jossey-Bass.

Saxe, G. B. (1991) *Culture and cognitive development: Studies in mathematical understanding*. Hillsdale, NJ: Lawrence Erlbaum.

Schmidt, W. H., Jorde, D., Cogan, L. S., Barrier, E., Gonzalo, I., Moser, U., Shimizu, K., Sawada, To., Balverde, B. A., McKnight, C., Prawat, R. S., Wiley, D. E., Raizen, S. A., Gritton, E. D., Wolfe, R. G. (1996). *Characterizing pedagogical flow: An investigation of mathematics and science teaching in six countries*. Dordrecht, The Netherlands: Kluwer Academic Publishers.

Schmidt, W. H., McKnight, C. C., Cogan, L. S., Jakwerth, P. M., & Houang, R. T. (1999). *Facing the consequences: Using TIMSS for a closer look at U.S. mathematics and science education*. Dordrecht, The Netherlands: Kluwer Academic Publishers.

Schmidt, W. H., McKnight, C. C., Raizen, S. (1997a). *A splintered vision: An investigation of U.S. science and mathematics education*. Dordrecht, The Netherlands: Kluwer Academic Publishers.

Schmidt, W. H., McKnight, C. C., & Raizen, S. (1997b). *A splintered vision: An investigation of U.S. science and mathematics education*. Executive summary [On-line]. Retrieved November 1999 from the World Wide Web: http: ustimss.msu.edu/splintrd.pdf

Schmidt, W. H., McKnight, C.C., Valverde, G. A., Houang, R. T., & Wiley, D. E. (1997). *Many visions, many aims: Volume 12, a cross-national investigation of curricular intentions in school mathematics*. Dordrecht, The Netherlands: Kluwer Academic Publishers.

Schnur, J. O., & Lang, J. W. (1976). Just pushing buttons or learning? A case for minicalculators. *Arithmetic Teacher, 23*, 559–562.

Schwatt, I. J. (1910). On the curriculum of mathematics. *The Mathematics Teacher, 3*, 1–8.

Scriven, M. (1967). The methodology of evaluation. In R. W. Tyler, R. M. Gagne, & M. Scriven, (Eds.), *AERA Monograph Series on Curriculum Evalaution: No. 1. Perspectives of curriculum evaluation* (pp. 39–82). Chicago: Rand McNally.

Shimahara, N. K. (1998). The Japanese model of professional development: Teaching as a craft. *Teaching and Teacher Education, 14*, 451–462.

Shimahara, N. K., & Sakai, A. (1995). *Learning to teach in two cultures: Japan and the United States*. New York: Garland.

Siegler, R. S., & Stern, E. (1998). Conscious and unconscious strategy discoveries: A microgenetic analysis. *Journal of Experimental Psychology: General, 127*(4), 377–398.

Silbert, J., Carnine, D., and Stein, M. (1981). *Direct instruction mathematics*. Columbus, OH: Merrill.

Silver, E. A. (1997, February). "Algebra for all." Increasing students' access to algebraic ideas, not just algebra courses. *Mathematics teaching in the middle school, 2*(4), 204–207.

Smith, M. L., & Glass, G. V. (1987). *Research and evaluation in education and the social sciences.* Englewood Cliffs, NJ: Prentice Hall.

Snyder, J., Bolin, F., & Zumwalt, K. (1992). Curriculum implementation. In P.W. Jackson (Ed.), *Handbook of research on curriculum* (pp. 402–435). New York: Macmillan.

Sommerfeld, M. (1996, 24 April). Calif. parents target math frameworks. *Education Week* [On-line]. Retrieved November 1999 from the World Wide Web: http://www.edweek.org/

SRA/McGraw-Hill. (1991). *Connecting Math Concepts.* New York: Author.

Stallings, J. (1979). *How to change the process of teaching basic reading skills in secondary schools: Executive summary.* Menlo Park, CA: SRI International.

Stallings, J. (1980). Allocated academic learning time revisited, or beyond time on task. *Educational Researcher, 9,* 11–16.

Standifer, C. E., & Maples, E. G. (1981). Achievement and attitude of third-grade students in using two types of calculators. *School Science and Mathematics, 81,* 17–24.

Starkey, P. (1983). *Some precursors of early arithmetic competencies.* Paper presented at the Biennial Meeting of the Society for Research in Child Development, Detroit, MI.

Steen, L. A. (1992, April). Does everybody need to study algebra? *The Mathematics Teacher, 85* (4), 258–260.

Stein, M., Silbert, J., & Carnine, D. (1997). *Designing effective mathematics instruction: A direct instruction approach.* Upper Saddle River, NJ: Merrill.

Stein, S. K. (1996). *Strength in numbers: Discovering the joy and power of mathematics in everyday life.* New York: John Wiley.

Stevenson, H. W., & Stigler,. J. W. (1992). *The learning gap.* New York: Summit Books.

Stigler, J. W., & Hiebert, J. (1997, January). Understanding and improving classroom mathematics instruction: An overview of the TIMSS video study. *Phi Delta Kappan,* 14–21.

Stigler, J. W., & Hiebert, J. (1999). *The teaching gap.* New York: The Free Press.

Stone, J. E., & Clements, A. (1998). Research and innovation: Let the buyer beware. In R.R. Spillane & P. Regnier (Eds.), *The superintendent of the future* (pp. 59–97). Gaithersburg, MD: Aspen Publishers.

Sutaria, S. D. (1985). *Specific learning disabilities: Nature and needs.* Springfield, IL: Charles C. Thomas.

Sweller, J., Mawer, R. F., & Ward, M. R. (1983). Development of expertise in mathematical problem solving. *Journal of Experimental Psychology: General. 112,* 639–661.

Symonds, P. M., & Chase, D. H. (1929). Practice vs. motivation. *Journal of Educational Psychology, 20,* 19–35.

Theophrastus (278 b.c.). (1968). In E. M. Beck (Ed.), *Bartlett's familiar quotations* (14th ed., p. 104). Boston: Little, Brown.

Thiessen, D., & Matthias, M. (1992). *The wonderful world of mathematics: A critically annotated list of children's book in mathematics.* Reston, VA: National Council of Teachers of Mathematics.

Thyer, D., & Maggs, J. (1991). *Teaching mathematics to young children.* London: Casell Educational Limited.

Thornton, C. A. (1978). Emphasizing thinking strategies in basic fact instruction. *Journal for Research in Mathematics Education, 9,* 214–227.

Thyer, D., and Maggs, J. (1991). *Teaching mathematics to young children.* London: Casell Educational Limited.

TIMSS International Study Center. (1997). *About TIMSS & TIMSS-Repeat* [On-line]. Author. Retrieved November, 1999 from the World Wide Web: http://www.csteep.bc.edu/timms

University of Chicago School Mathematics Project. (1992). *Japanese grade 7 mathematics. Japanese grade 8 mathematics. Japanese grade 9 mathematics.* Chicago: Author.

University of Chicago School Mathematics Project. (1992). *Russian grade 1 mathematics. Russian grade 2 mathematics. Russian grade 3 mathematics.* Chicago: Author.

U.S. Department of Commerce. (1999). *America's new deficit: The shortage of information technology workers* [On-line]. Washington, DC: Office of Technology Policy, U.S. Department of Commerce. Retrieved November, 1999 from the World Wide Web in portable document file (PDF) format: http://www.ta.doc.gov/report/itsw/itsw.pdf.

U.S. Department of Education. (1997). *Mathematics equals opportunity* [On-line]. White paper prepared for U.S. Secretary of Education Richard W. Riley. Washington, DC: U.S. Department of Education. Retrieved November, 1999 from the World Wide Web in portable document file (PDF) format: http://ed.gov/pubs/math

U.S. Department of Education. (1998). *Education at a glance: OECD* [Organization for Economic Cooperation and Development] *indicators 1998.* National Center for Education Statistics.

U.S. Department of Education. (1999). *Attaining Excellence: A TIMMS resource kit (#065-000-01013-5).* Pittsburgh, PA: U.S. Government Printing Office.

U.S. Department of Education. (in press). *Analysis of NELS: 88 follow-up data: factors that affect college enrollment.* Washington, DC: U.S. Department of Education Planning and Evaluation Service.

U.S. Department of Education. Office of Educational Research and Improvement. (1999). *Highlights from TIMSS. Overview and key findings across grade levels.* Author. Retrieved November, 1999 from the World Wide Web in portable document file (PDF) format: http://nces.ed.gov/timms

U.S. Department of Education's Mathematics and Science Expert Panel. (1999). *Exemplary & Promising Mathematics Programs.* U.S. Department of Education. Retrieved November 1999 from the World Wide Web in portable document file (PDF) format: http://enc.org/ed/exemplary/

U.S. Department of Labor, Bureau of Labor Statistics. (1997). National Longitudinal Survey of Youth, 1979–93. *Education and the Economy: An Indicators Report.* Washington, DC: National Center for Education Statistics, U.S. Department of Education.

Usiskin, Z. (1994, August). What changes should be made for the 2nd edition of the NCTM Standards? *Humanistic Mathematics Network Journal, 10,* 13–38.

Venezky, R. L., & Winfield, L. F. (1979). *Schools that succeed beyond expectations in reading.* Studies in Education. Newark, NJ: University of Delaware. ERIC Accession No. ED 177 484.

Viadero, D. (1999, June 23). What is and isn't research? *Education Week,* pp. 33–36.

von Glaserfeld, E. (1995). *Radical constructivism.* London: The Falmer Press.

von Glaserfeld, E., & Steffe, L. P. (1991). Conceptual models in educational research and practice. *Journal of Educational Thought, 25,* 91–103.

Watson, B. (1967). Basic writings of Mo Tzu, Hsun Tzu, and Han Fei Tzu. New York: Columbia University Press.

West, P. (1995, June 7). Palo Alto parents square off over math curriculum. [On-line]. *Education Week.* Retrieved November, 1999 from the World Wide Web: http://www.edweek.org

WestEd. (1997). *Schoolwide reform: A new outlook (vols. 1 & 2).* San Francisco, CA: Author.

Wu, Hung-Hsi. (1997). The mathematics education reform: Why you should be concerned and what you can do. *American Mathematical Monthly, 104,* 946–954.

Wu, Hung-Hsi. (1999). Basic skills versus conceptual undersanding: A bogus dichotomy in mathematics education. *American Educator, 23*(3), 14–18, 51.

Yoshida, M. (1999, December). *Lesson study: A case study of a Japanese approach to improving instruction through school-based teacher development.* Unpublished doctoral dissertation, University of Chicago.

Zemelman, S., Daniels, H., & Hyde, A. (1998). *Best practices: New standards for teaching and learning in America's schools.* Portsmouth, NH: Heinemann.

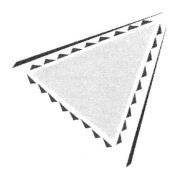

# Index